THE MARVELOUS PARTICIPATION

An Awesome Partnership with God

Written for New Converts
And Unfulfilled Believers
Who Desire to be Used by God in His Way

By Carol Price

The Marvelous Participation
An Awesome Partnership with God
Carol Price

Published by Austin Brothers Publishing, Fort Worth, Texas
www.abpbooks.com

ISBN 978-0-9996328-8-8
Copyright © 2018 by Carol Price

Unless otherwise indicated, all Scripture quotations are taken from the Holy Bible, New Living Translation, copyright © 1996, 2004, 2007, 2013, 2015 by Tyndale House Foundation. Used by permission of Tyndale House Publishers, Inc., Carol Stream, Illinois 60188. All rights reserved.

Abbreviated list of gift descriptions used by permission of Ministry Tools Resource Center https://MinTools.com/gifts-list.htm

ALL RIGHTS RESERVED. No part of this book may be reproduced in any form without permission in writing from the publisher, except in the case of brief quotations embodied in critical reviews or articles.

Printed in the United States of America
2018 -- First Edition

ACKNOWLEDGMENTS

*My deepest gratitude —
To Sharon Jackson of Hanford, California, who encouraged me in 2011 to write this book*

To my good friend, Susan Warren Jackson, for her faithfulness in giving me suggestions on how to improve the language and flow of this manuscript

To Leon Revels who inspected this manuscript for biblical correctness and relevance

To my family and friends in California and Texas who, in various ways, encouraged me over the long haul to complete this work.

To Jeremy Bishop of Unspash.com whose photo adorns the cover.

Contents

Foreword	1
Introduction	3
PART 1: MIRA'S STORY	7
Chapter 1: The Battle for A Soul	9
Chapter 2: But God Had A Plan	21
Chapter 3: His Plan Includes Emotional Healing	25
PART 2: Who are People Meant to Be	31
Chapter 4: Who People Were Not Meant To Be	33
Chapter 5: Made in His Image	37
Chapter 6: Attributes People Can Mirror	39
Chapter 7: The Onion Example	47
Chapter 8: Consider the Fate of the Immortal Spirit	51
Chapter 9: Does God Really See Me?	55
Chapter 10: Preparing to Participate with God	61
PART 3: What Are Believers Meant To Do?	65
Chapter 11: A Change of Focus	67
Chapter 12: It's All about Love	71
Chapter 13: Every Believer Has a Specific Calling	77
Chapter 14: Gifted to Serve Others	81
Chapter 15: You Are Unique	87
Chapter 16: How to Recognize Your Design	91
Chapter 17: Some Gift Examples	99
PART 4: Your Calling Is Already Yours!	105
Chapter 18: Does Your Perspective Need to Change?	107

Chapter 19: Love Yourself	111
PART 5: Strong Warnings	115
Chapter 20: Don't Lose Focus	117
PART 6: The Marvelous Participation	121
Chapter 21: Summing It Up	123
Abbreviated List Of Gift Descriptions	127
Suggestions For Further Reading	131

Foreword

In the New Testament, the term *believers* refers to those who have been redeemed and begun a relationship with God by receiving Jesus as Savior and Lord. The result of a personal salvation experience is that they entrust, or commit, their material and spiritual well-being to Jesus and what He promised, both in this world and for eternity. They enter a covenant with God through the shed blood of Jesus, the Savior.

Believers have confidence in the truth that Jesus is both Savior and God. They have experienced sorrow for sin and repented. They receive forgiveness from God and are delivered from the power of sin to rule their lives. In other words, they are saved.

The effect of their salvation is that they are new creatures in Christ and members of the spiritual Body of Christ. From that time forward, believers are actively involved in growing in the knowledge of who God is, growing in the fruit of His Spirit, and submitting to His rule in their lives.

There is more. I recently heard a church member remark that she wanted to glorify God, but she was waiting to hear from Him how she could be used in His service after He figured it out. I don't know if she was serious or speaking in jest. Either way, her comment points to confusion about God's calling on our lives.

This book is written to encourage new converts to start their journey with God from a more informed perspective. It is also written to believers who have, up to now, not lived each day in the power, freedom from fear, joy, peace, and fulfillment, promised to them by God. Hopefully, by the end of this book, the minds and spirits of readers will have been encouraged to believe they have been designed by God for specific service.

It is also important to distinguish between those who have been redeemed through a personal salvation experience and those who decided to join a church out of fear or from a sense of duty. In consideration of the focus of this book, the term *believer* does not apply to those in the second group if they have not been saved and are not yet in covenant with God through Jesus, the Savior.

If you are redeemed and have committed your life to God, please know that He has designed you for a specific area of service and that He wants to equip you to work with Him in a most marvelous way.

Introduction

THE MARVELOUS PARTICIPATION

That's why, when I heard of the solid trust you have in the Master Jesus and your outpouring of love to all the Christians, I couldn't stop thanking God for you—everytime I prayed, I'd think of you and give thanks. But I do more than thank. I ask—ask the God of our Master, Jesus Christ, the God of glory— to make you intelligent and discerning in knowing him personally, your eyes focused and clear, so that you can see exactly what it is he is calling you to do, grasp the immensity of this glorious way of life he has for Christians, oh, the utter extravagance of his work in us who trust him—endless energy, boundless strength! Ephesians 1:15-19a (The Message)

A definition of the word *marvelous* is "something to be wondered at." It is marvelous that a fallible human being can be invited by God to join with Him in His ministry of transforming lives.

Because of Jesus, believers can *dwell in the presence of God* every moment of each day. As we submit to God's rule in our lives, He enables us to participate in His life-changing ministry. He gives understanding about His kingdom and about how He has designed us to join Him in ministering to the needs of others.

We learn these things from Bible study and the counsel of the Holy Spirit. At a time of His choosing, God made Himself known through the ministry of Jesus so that people could clearly see His love in action. As we grow in knowledge and align ourselves with God, He shines through us as He did with Jesus and reveals the power of His love and mercy to others.

I am a believer who was shown by God how I fit into His plan. My journey of learning how to participate with God began when He planted a seed of thought in my mind. It happened like this: I awoke one morning with the words THINK BIG resounding in my mind. It was as though those words were positioned just above my forehead. They could not have had a greater impact if they had actually been spoken aloud by someone in the room.

Until that time, I had not been thinking big about God, about His power to do whatever He desires. Those two words drew me into a journey of discovery about *who* God intended for people to be and *what* people are meant to do. Through my journey, I learned that before I was born, God had a plan for who I should become. Before I was conceived, His plan took into account everything concerning my design such as who my parents would be, my gender, level of intelligence, nationality, and my place in society. I learned that I was designed with particular talents, skills, and abilities that would enable me to offer a specific service to others.

What a different impact the Body of Believers would have if

all or even most believers would come to understand how they have been designed for service and then faithfully work with God to accomplish His purposes. This would influence others to do the same—to focus on who they are meant to be and what they are meant to do in this life.

Another vital concept I learned is the profound impact of the war waged by Satan as he schemes to keep people from living the life God designed for each of us.

Do you know what God's plan is for your life? If not, He will enlighten you when you are ready to hear.

At first, what you learn might seem impossible. His plan for you might be frightening. But God asks you to have courage and trust Him.

He is asking you now to begin to THINK BIG! It's something you may never have done before.

You might ask, THINK BIG about what exactly?

THINK BIG about God. . . .

About who He is.

About all that He has done.

About what He wants to do now and in the future.

About what He wants to accomplish through you.

As you read on, ask yourself three questions:
- Why was I born?
- Am I growing into who God meant for me to be?
- What does God intend to accomplish through me?

Also, consider the following:
- About what are you thinking small?
- Is your focus mainly on your struggles?
- How would THINKING BIG change your perspective on your struggles?
- God sees everything and everybody all of the time. He loves you, He sees you, He knows your name.
- He keeps His promises.

This book discusses some of the things I learned about how God works. I thank God that my perspective is aligning more and more with His perspective. He has the power to completely change a life. His power can overcome any devastation that the evil of this world brings into our lives. I pray that these words will ignite a fire in you that will change your perspective about Who GOD IS, and who you are meant to be, and what you are meant to do.

God is awesome! It is an awesome privilege to work with Him. You can become a participant in His awesome work. It is what He most desires for you.

PART 1

Mira's Story

Stay alert! Watch out for your great enemy, the devil. He prowls around like a roaring lion, looking for someone to devour. 1 Peter 5:8

Chapter 1
The Battle for A Soul

Mira suffered three major traumas that could have caused her to lead a mediocre, defeated life beset by continual inner struggles. But God used her bad experiences as part of His plan for her life. The wisdom of God and His timing are perfect. He made Himself known to her at a time of His choosing and changed the direction of her life. She is no longer at the mercy of the evil influences in this world. I will use Mira's story to illustrate the power of God to overcome any hindrance and dramatically change the direction of a life from a path of defeat to one of godly purpose and victory.

We all have an enemy. His name is Satan. He is also known as the spirit of evil and the prince of this world. The Bible depicts him as an angelic being who usurped the earthly rule given by God to mankind. In doing so, he exposed himself as the enemy of God and humanity.

The immortal spirit of every person born into this world comes from God, and He has a call on the life of everyone. Satan's unrelenting plan is to keep people from fulfilling their godly purpose and to eternally separate us from God. He will use any means to accomplish this. He does not necessarily need to snuff out our physical lives in order to defeat God's plan for each of us. In fact, he'd rather corrupt our hopes and dreams, fill us with fear, selfishness, and greed, because then he wins if we willingly choose to reject God's will for our lives. Satan's purpose is to prevent people from living as God intended for us to live. When Satan causes people to distrust God or to not believe in God at all, he wins.

In Mira's case, Satan's plan was to rob her of self-worth, to move her into a depression, and, in the process, to divert her from knowing God. It is unfortunate that Satan can use people to aid him in carrying out his plan. He uses those who are vulnerable to his influence, and he does not care if a person has the title of Christian. He will use anyone he can. He is good at using people who are closest to us, such as family and friends, to bring about division and to create an atmosphere of distrust.

The one big hurdle that had to be overcome in Mira's adult life was the emotional damage she suffered as a child. Those who were closest to her unwittingly created an emotionally painful atmosphere that caused her to feel like she had no value. Coming to believe that she mattered to no one worked great devastation in her life.

> *The greatest loss is not loss of life.*
> *The greatest loss is what dies inside of us*
> *while we live.*
> Norman Cousins

Satan works tirelessly to bring about this type of living death in people. His plan for Mira was to break her down emotionally to the point where she would become complacent and depressed, with no hope and no expectations living a ruined life until she died without a relationship with God.

As you read her story, you will find Mira's experiences to be either more or less destructive than yours. However, I am sure that you will find some common elements from your own experiences with which you can relate.

HER STORY

Mira started out as a gutsy, fun-loving, sociable person. While her father was away serving in the Army, she and her mother lived with her maternal grandparents. As an only child for the first three years of her life, she loved interacting with other children.

A couple of times she left home and walked away, unnoticed, to make her way to a friend's home where there were other children with whom she could play. The friend lived several blocks away, but because she and her mother had walked there periodically to visit, Mira was able to remember the way. Two times she managed to get there without getting lost. Her mother would eventually notice she was missing, and after searching, would find her at the friend's house. A strong scolding after the second time stopped Mira from wandering away again. Her mother seemed unconcerned that Mira didn't like playing alone. But even when she did have to be alone, she was able to enjoy herself. The grandparents' back yard was an interesting and fun place where at one time or another there were rabbits, geese, hens, a rooster, and a vegetable garden.

There came a time when things changed drastically. Mira's father came home after being discharged from the Army, and that was the beginning of ongoing trouble for her. Mira's first memory of feeling unwanted happened not long after his return. There was only one bedroom in their apartment on the second floor of her grandparents' home, and her bed was in the same room as her parents' bed. One night when Mira's mother went out for the evening to a club meeting, Mira was in her bed crying because she missed her mother. Her father, with great exasperation about her crying, roughly grabbed her up. After tossing her onto their bed, he laid down, turning his back to her. Wanting to be comforted, Mira tried to snuggle up next to his back. He uttered something harsh and roughly pushed her away. Having been accustomed to affection from her mother and grandparents, she was shocked by his anger and rough handling.

It was downhill from there, but her mother didn't seem to notice that something was wrong. Mira changed from being outgoing and fun-loving into a quiet, subdued child. Two years later Mira's brother was born, and she watched her father treat him with love. Three years after that Mira's sister was born, and she watched her father treat the new baby with love. Mira understood that her father didn't like her, but she didn't know the reason. It wasn't until she was fifty years old that she learned why her father had treated her with such cold disdain. He didn't believe she was his daughter. It didn't matter that she looked like him and other members of his family. His own mother could see the family resemblance. For whatever reason, he could not bring himself to own her as his.

After Mira saw the *Cinderella* movie, she noticed their situations were somewhat similar. Cinderella was also treated as an outsider and largely ignored. However, while Cinderella had a sunny, positive disposition, Mira was moody and angry. Many years later she saw her second-grade class picture. It showed a very sad, unanimated child. After she was saved, a prophet of God told Mira that when she was born, her mother had experienced difficult times.

As an adult, Mira came to understand how three childhood traumas dramatically shaped her life. The first trauma was the broken bond between her and her mother, who failed to protect her and who offered no training or direction as she grew up. At first, although Mira didn't understand why her father was allowed to treat her like he did, she continued to trust her mother. Mira's trust was finally broken by what happened the summer after he rejoined the family.

The fun and interesting back yard became even more so after Mira's mother gave her a puppy. Each morning Mira awoke with enthusiasm and rushed to get dressed and have breakfast so that she could go outside to play with her puppy. One morning she ran outside to find him, and he wasn't there. After questioning her mother, Mira was told that the puppy had gotten sick and had to be taken away. She was crushed. The puppy had been a friend, and all of a sudden, he was gone without warning.

One morning soon after that as her mother was leaving home, Mira asked where she was going. Her mother's response was that she was going to see a man about a dog. Oh, boy, was Mira excited! She thought she was going to get another puppy.

But her mother came home empty-handed, and Mira was disappointed. Soon after, her mother again stated that she was going to see a man about a dog, and once again came home without a puppy. Mira was not only disappointed, but she felt a growing anger and distrust of her mother. She felt betrayed by what seemed a string of broken promises about a dog, and under that pain lay an undercurrent much deeper—an anger about how her father was allowed to treat her, unchecked by her mother who was supposed to protect her.

Many years later, Mira learned that the phrase going to see a man about a dog was her mother's way of telling her that where she was going was none of Mira's business. Her mother didn't mean to tell a lie or set Mira up for a hope for a friend only to be continually disappointed. Her mother just thought it was a cute thing to say. But by the time Mira understood this miscommunication that had caused her much hurt and sorrow, she was in the grip of a strong resentment toward her mother.

A second trauma Mira faced as a child was of being an outcast among other children from the neighborhood and at school. After Mira's brother and sister were born, her mother began to work outside of the home. Eventually the five members of the family moved out of her grandparents' house and into their own home where Mira had her own bedroom. She began to wet the bed, and she thinks this went on for about a year. Mira doesn't remember how often her bedding was changed, but she clearly remembers it wasn't often enough. During the summer, she could raise a window to air out her room, which smelled strongly of urine. But during the winter, there was no relief from the smell coming from a ruined mattress. Mira slept in her underwear. At night, she would wet the bed, get up in the morning, and not wash herself or change her underwear. The bedroom stank, and so did she. Sometimes flies and gnats would swarm in her room.

One evening her parents hired a babysitter while they went out. The babysitter came into Mira's bedroom, became horrified at the stench, and never came back. During that same period, Mira remembered going to the YMCA to watch a play that was being put on for the neighborhood children. She had wet the bed during the night and had not changed her underwear before leaving home. She stank. The other children who sat around her at the play noticed, of course, and the teasing began in earnest. Mira was taunted by the children in her neighborhood and at school. The day of the play was the day that Mira began to feel dirty, and unwelcome, and friendless.

Mira's parents finally took her to a doctor to have the cause of her bed-wetting diagnosed. After examining her and asking some pertinent questions, the doctor told her parents that Mira's bed-wetting was not because of a physical problem. Rather, it was an act of rebellion, and the doctor suggested that, at the least, they should invest in a contraption to stop the bed-wetting. The contraption turned out to be a rubber sheet with a bell that rang at the first bit of moisture. After being awakened by the bell several times, Mira learned to wake up and use the bathroom instead of wetting the bed. But even after that, she still had a hygiene problem, because she had not been taught how to clean herself properly and she was too depressed to care. Because she was unpleasant to be near due to poor hygiene and because she had no friends, she was not socialized as a child and didn't learn how to productively interact with others during her crucial formative years.

Why didn't Mira's mother help her? She still doesn't know why her mother and father were unable to function as loving parents. She only knows that what the prophet said about her mother was true.

Eventually Mira's hygiene improved. But a third trauma occurred. She felt threatened in her own home. As she matured, Mira began to feel afraid, though she could not explain why. It was years later that she came to understand the cause of her fear. Using her experience as an adult, Mira understood that she had felt stalked. However, it was more than that. Her memory is dim, but there were fragmented incidents she could recall of her father touching her in ways that she felt were wrong. She reported the touching to her mother who must have confronted her father, because he stopped bothering her physically. But her fear continued for years. From around the age of ten until she was in her late teens, Mira didn't feel safe in her home, and resentment toward her mother increased. Without protection and structure, Mira was pretty much on her own most of the time.

One summer when Mira was sixteen years old, her mother announced that she was going to start working a night shift. Fearful of having her mother away from home at night, Mira begged her several times not to take the job. But, as usual, her mother paid no attention to Mira's needs. Her mother simply said that taking this job was something she needed to do for herself.

After her mother started working nights, Mira would leave home on weekday evenings and stay out until she was sure that her father was asleep. During that time, she met someone in a park near her house who seduced her, and she became pregnant with her first child, a daughter. Starved for love, Mira was vulnerable to anyone who paid attention to her. She was sorely neglected and unprepared to face life in a productive way. What she remembers learning from her mother was how to say "please" and "thank you," and that lesson was merely by example.

After Mira's parents learned she was expecting a child, her mother and siblings moved with her to another state where the grandparents had relocated, leaving her father behind. Mira was overjoyed, because she thought they were finally getting away from him. She didn't realize that he had stayed behind only until their house was sold. He then followed them to their new home, and her turmoil continued. After three years, Mira was pregnant again. According to her father, her choices at that point were to keep the baby and be put out of the house, or to place the baby for adoption. The baby, a son, was adopted by a close relative.

Mira's mother was unable to give her direction about anything. Her resentment toward her mother was ongoing, and her contempt for her father continued. Eventually, Mira met someone after graduating high school and moved to his home state to be with him. Being unacquainted with what it means to love and care for others, Mira felt nothing about leaving her daughter behind with her mother. She was a sweet baby, but Mira had not learned to care for herself and didn't know how to care for a child. How ironic it is to her now, that she had left her beautiful daughter with the same people who had worked such destruction in her own life. This is a sorrow that Mira will carry all of her life. She can relate to King David, who said,

> *For I know my transgressions, and (the consequences of) my sin is always before me.*
> *Psalm 51:3 (NIV) (paraphrased)*

Mira's daughter and her son who had been adopted suffered from her abandonment and still feel its effects. Words of apology are not enough when she witnesses the emotional struggles that affect their lives. However, she continues to hope that with God's help, her daughter and son will heal from their emotional damage and begin a relationship with Him.

Years later, Mira learned some things that helped her understand what drove her fear of being home alone with her father. She overheard one of her aunts talk about how her father had tried to sexually molest another aunt. Mira learned of another incident that occurred after her father and mother divorced. He married a woman who had two teenage daughters. He eventually was asked to leave their home, because one of the daughters accused him of trying to molest her. As an adult, Mira understood that her father had a strong, lustful spirit. Even after he stopped bothering her physically, it was his spirit that made her feel stalked and frightened for years. The world is full of the various manifestations of lustful spirits that work to ruin people's lives.

Mira doesn't believe that her parents intended to harm her, but their actions and extreme neglect wrought great destruction in her. She could have become a drug addict or an alcoholic, or she could have committed suicide. Looking back, she can see how Satan's evil influence could have trapped her in life-long hopelessness. She could have been eternally lost after having lived a tormented life.

Chapter 2
But God Had A Plan

For I know the plans I have for you, says the LORD. They are plans for good and not for disaster, to give you a future and a hope.
Jeremiah 29:11

Mira was caught up in a spiritual battle for her soul. As an adult, it looked like Satan was winning the battle because Mira was unaware of God and couldn't ask for His help. Inwardly, she felt valueless, mildly depressed, and ashamed about her past. Despite how she perceived herself, Mira felt the need to present a good face to others.

She eventually married and birthed another son. She appeared to be living a good life with a family, a decent income, and no unmet material needs. However, the atmosphere in her home was not good, because Satan was at work causing division and distrust in the lives of her family members. In the midst of the messiness, Mira came to recognize God's plan for her as it began to unfold in the chaos.

The day came when God captured her attention and gave her a life-changing experience. What Satan had worked so hard to prevent came to pass. The Holy Spirit led her to Jesus, and Jesus saved her. God began to undo the emotional damage of her past. The contradiction between what was going on inside of her and the face she presented to the world began to fade as God's presence worked to dramatically change her beliefs, and in the process, her life. Satan had lost the battle!

As the Holy Spirit began to instruct Mira in godly living, He had her to understand that although she had gone through many devastating experiences, He had been with her all along the way. He taught her about the ongoing battle between good and evil, and He limited the force of what came against her. Through His guidance, she gained wisdom and understanding of the cause and effects of her bad experiences. As her knowledge increased, God began to use her as a source of encouragement and healing for other hurting people that He placed within her sphere of influence. Because of what she had gone through, she was able to have compassion and empathy for others who were emotionally damaged. Those people listened to Mira, and trusted her, because she too had experienced trauma. Now she can joyfully say along with the Apostle Paul, *All praise to God, the Father of our Lord Jesus Christ. God is our merciful Father and the source of all comfort. He comforts us in all our troubles so that we can comfort others. When they are troubled, we will be able to give them the same comfort God has given us.* (2 Corinthians 1:3-4)

Several years after Mira was saved, her youngest son died. In the midst of her profound grief, God gave Mira two precious promises. He let her know that her son, who had passed on, is safe with Him, and He has salvation plans for her other children, grandchildren, and a great-grandchild. He told her that He will safeguard her and everything that concerns her. Their lives are not trouble-free, but Mira knows that God is in control and will keep His promises.

Chapter 3
His Plan Includes Emotional Healing

But He was wounded for our transgressions, He was bruised for our guilt and iniquities; the chastisement [needful to obtain] peace and well-being for us was upon Him, and with the stripes [that wounded] Him we are healed and made whole.
Isaiah 53:5 (AMP)

The Apostle Paul urged believers to be transformed by the renewing of their minds (Romans 12:1-2). The transformation process includes the healing of emotional pain. Mira was much in need of healing from the traumas she suffered during her formative years. Her healing began when God saved her. It was easy for God to cleanse her spirit by means of His indwelling presence. The difficult part was the renewing of her mind to change her thinking.

Her thought patterns had become entrenched by the time God entered her heart. But no matter how difficult the struggle, Mira was determined to work with God as He helped her undo the habitual thought patterns formed by the atmosphere in which she had lived. As her mind was being renewed, she found the benefits of transformation to be well worth the struggle.

Before we are saved, we think like the world around us, which is under the control of Satan. After salvation, God helps us think and act like members of His kingdom. The internal struggle can be quite difficult, but if we stick with the process of Bible study, meditation, and prayer, emotional healing can become a reality.

Although the following is far from an in-depth discussion about emotional healing and forgiveness, there is a need to mention both.

Everybody has memories—some are good, some are not so good, and some are horrible. When children are emotionally wounded, they don't have an understanding of life that would enable them to objectively process their painful experiences. Lacking understanding, children may feel that what happened to them was their fault; that there was something wrong with them and therefore, they deserved what happened in some way. Their pain is often accompanied by guilt, shame, and deep-seated anger.

Because memories are embedded in our brains, healing can't be accomplished by wiping them out. Healing comes when the pain associated with bad memories is removed. Scars from the experiences may remain, but the memories themselves become merely facts of what happened in the past. The emotional responses no longer overwhelm.

True and lasting forgiveness, which is a divine work of God, is the key to removing the pain and negative effects of bad memories. Forgiveness is a choice that begins in the heart of a person. Forgiveness is enabled by the divine influence of the Holy Spirit. It is the act of letting go of the emotional baggage of guilt and offense that keeps us tied to the past. It is a release of anger and any bitterness or hatred produced by a grudge. Forgiveness sets the forgiver and others completely free of all negative emotions and allows the one who forgives to move forward in life.

God's Word and the Holy Spirit's divine influence on the heart give the believer the ability and power to reassess painful experiences from God's perspective. No one is better able to work forgiveness in us than God Himself, who is the author of forgiveness and redemption. Instead of automatically taking the blame or continuing to hold grudges against others, godly wisdom can enable a person to ask some pertinent questions such as:

What caused that which happened to be painful?

Was what happened due to a personal shortcoming of the believer, or were the painful experiences based on the shortcomings of others?

Were the actions of others done to intentionally inflict pain, or were their actions a result of their own unhealed wounds?

Even after forgiveness has been given, is a trusting relationship possible?

Filtering bad memories through a similar process can shift the focus from the pain to an objective attempt to understand its cause. Forgiveness does not always include a trusting relationship with the pain-giver. But as believers internalize Scripture and take on God's way of thinking, we accept that forgiveness of ourselves and others is mandatory.

An understanding of what caused others to do what they did is not always possible, but it is helpful to recognize that others have had their own painful experiences that helped shape their lives. However, whether or not we come to understand the reasons behind the actions of others, forgiveness is a necessary prerequisite for healing.

> *Forgiveness is the key to the heart's shackles.*
> Richard Paul Evans, <u>The Walk</u>

Revisiting her bad experiences as an adult gave Mira helpful insights. She had believed that the hurtful things she experienced were because there was something wrong with her. As an adult, she now knows there was something lacking in her parents, which was the true cause of those painful experiences. God has helped her to be merciful toward them because she now understands they must have suffered their own traumas. With His compassionate help, Mira was able to forgive them, and in the process, she was set free from deep-seated anger and guilt.

There are times when she experiences regrets because of her own failures as a parent, but because of her hope in God, she can move ahead and serve others with her whole heart. What a miracle it is when God helps us focus less on what was done to us and, instead, empathize with others who are suffering emotional pain.

Mira is only one among myriads of people whose lives have been torn up and nearly destroyed by despicable circumstances to the point where recovery seemed impossible. The destructive forces in the world have caused many to feel valueless and useless, thinking that they cannot possibly do anything productive or work for the good of others. The feelings that many take as truth are often only beliefs fostered by incorrect perceptions, which can cause people to miss the path destined for them by God.

Feelings can be deceptive. Even among believers, there are some who have served in some type of ministry but feel that now, because they are elderly, or weary, or sick, or disabled, their usefulness has passed. But it is not how we feel nor what we have gone through that determines the length and depth of our usefulness. When we accept God's will and calling on our lives, it is He who determines how we will be used for whatever length of time we are needed.

I once took part in a prayer seminar that was led by a deeply anointed, elderly lady. In order to conduct her prayer ministry, she traveled with a companion and an oxygen tank. She refused to allow the discomfort of her breathing disability to stop her from being used by God to bless others.

Our past or our weaknesses can cease to define us. As we accept God's will, it is He who defines us. As you come to see yourself through His eyes, the knowledge of how loved and valued you are will draw you closer to the One who is the lover of your soul.

You are leaving a lasting impression on someone. I learned this about myself from a member of my congregation. I felt insignificant until the day she told me that others were watching me; my demeanor and how I reacted to difficult situations. Her statement caused me to be more sensitive to my effect on those around me and more careful to leave a positive influence. Don't underestimate your power to influence others, positively or negatively. God has a plan for your life. Let Him show you how to live a life that will reflect Him. And always remember,

> *You are not who you **think** you are.*
> *You are not who people **think** you are.*
> *You are who God **says** you are!*

PART 2

Who Are People Meant To Be?

Chapter 4
Who People Were Not Meant To Be

The Bible tells us that mankind began in a pure state that was later corrupted by the sin of disobedience in the Garden of Eden. This event warns us to be watchful, because not only does humanity have to deal with a fallen nature but also with evil spirits who are active in the world. The fallen state of mankind is referenced in Ephesians 4:20-32 where believers are told to strip themselves of their worldly behaviors. The Apostle Paul referred to the temptations to lie, steal, hold anger, grudges, and bitterness toward others; to use foul, abusive language; to slander; and to exhibit any other type of evil behavior.

People were not created to be victims of the disharmonies that are of this world, such as physical and mental abuse, disease, depression, fear, sorrow, misery, poverty, and the trouble that flows from all of these. People were not meant to cause or experience wretchedness of any kind, but because of the nature of sin and ongoing disobedience to God, these things continue to be part of our lives.

A common failure of people is judging, which Jesus warns us against doing in Matthew 7:1-2. To judge is to condemn. All too often believers form opinions about the actions of others based on little or no information. Jesus cautions us: if we condemn others, we will be condemned by the same standard we use against them. When believers see this as truth, we are careful not to condemn others, but instead, to pray for them if a change of behavior is needed.

There is a difference between being judgmental and using good judgment. Believers are expected to use good judgment in making decisions based on what we learn from God. Even though we may be aware of the failings of others, we do not have the right to denigrate another's value as a human being created by God. Although the **acts** of others may be construed as worthless, no one has enough knowledge or the authority to speak of anyone as **being** worthless.

God loves everybody, but He does not condone the evil that people do. While we also should not excuse evil, we must be careful that we don't fall into the trap of being judgmental. God does not look favorably upon those who say or do things that demean the value of human beings made in His image. Life is tough and full of traps into which anyone can fall. Evil influences, hatred, and abuse might cause anyone to do horrible things. If we take an honest look at ourselves and what we might be capable of if we had to live the despicable lives some are forced to endure, we can see the horrible things done by others and say, "There but for the grace of God go I."

Consider the Bible verses that speak of those who were despised by their neighbors but were treated with mercy and grace by Jesus, who knew their heart and their future. Wherever possible, be mindful of using compassion and the mercy of Jesus with others and leaving judgment to Him.

There will come a time when everybody will be judged (2 Corinthians 5:10). Only God knows the future. Those who have committed the most heinous crimes may receive forgiveness from God before they die. Dare we condemn someone who may one day repent and be forgiven? Rather than focusing on condemnation, shouldn't we focus on what Jesus taught about love? If God loves everybody unconditionally, shouldn't we strive to do the same? God's kind of love is a powerful force that can change the hearts of others in spite of the ugliness of sin in the world. Instead of continuing to exhibit worldly behavior, believers are expected to grow in character, use good judgment in everyday living, and become examples of the mercy and grace of God.

Chapter 5
Made in His Image

So all of us who have had that veil removed can see and reflect the glory of the Lord. And the Lord—who is the Spirit—makes us more and more like him as we are changed into his glorious image.
2 Corinthians 3:18

Have you recognized the wonder of being made in the image of God? And even though His image has been blurred by sin, it has not been erased in mankind. This underscores the fact that every person who has been, or who will be born, has intrinsic value. It does not matter where a person is born, or what a person looks like, or how a person has lived. This fundamental truth includes everybody.

Something else becomes clear once we internalize how God created us. The Bible teaches that humanity has its roots in two people, Adam and Eve. This means that there are not many races of people. There is only one race, which is the human race. Mankind is one race with many nations, separated by tribalism. No nation is any better or worse than another. The same general characteristics can be found in people anywhere in the world. We can find people with similar personalities, ways of expressing love, or those who are full of hatred. We can find people with various levels of intelligence. There are those who love God, those who deny His existence, and those who believe in other gods. Some people strive for power above all else, and others work unselfishly for the good of their neighbors. The overriding factor is that sin infected everybody, and it is only through the cleansing that comes with salvation through Jesus that any of us can have a relationship with God and begin the journey back to who we were meant to be—people who mirror His image.

Chapter 6
Attributes People Can Mirror

Even if we thoroughly studied the Bible from beginning to end, it would still be impossible to know everything about God. However, if we believe in His supremacy, it becomes evident that humans cannot fully mirror who He is because some attributes are His alone. Three qualities that belong only to God are His omnipotence, omnipresence, and omniscience.

God is all-powerful, able to be everywhere at the same time, and has complete and unlimited knowledge of everything He created. He is never unaware or surprised about what is going on anywhere in His universe and in this world. I repeat, everything is known to Him. There are no chance incidents or accidental happenings. He is in control of EVERYTHING, at ALL TIMES, the good, the bad, and the ugly. He does not cause evil behavior, but He is always in control of its limits. These three attributes are what make God's ways too much for mankind to fully comprehend because only He can see the big picture.

The Bible tells us that God is Love. He gave humans the ability to reflect His love. The ways that people reflect the attribute of love are interesting. Following is a list recognized by ancient philosophers of what humans call love, and they can be used to highlight the wonder of the love of God.

Eros was named after the Greek god of fertility. *Eros* represented sexual passion and desire. He was not always thought of as a positive figure because what he represented was viewed as a dangerous and irrational form of love that could lead to a loss of control. These days we could call this lust. *Eros* can die or move on when feelings change and lust is no longer satisfied.

Philia was a type of friendship love. *Philia* represented a comradely friendship exhibited by loyalty, sacrifice, and sharing of emotions. A different kind of *philia* was called *storge,* which described the love between parents and their children. *Philia* and *storge* can die or move from one person to another when feelings of betrayal, disappointment, or a loss of respect are present.

Ludus represented a playful love displayed as affection between children or among young lovers who flirted and teased one another. This kind of love can die or move from one person to another, based on whether or not feelings are satisfied.

Pragma represented the deep understanding that could develop between long-married couples. *Pragma* was exhibited by the showing of patience, compromise, and tolerance, to produce a productive relationship. Though more substantial than the previous three, this kind of love can also die based on a change in feelings.

Narcissism was named after the Greek god Narcissus. This was an erotic type of selfish gratification derived from personal admiration of physical or mental attributes and regarded only the person's own happiness or advantage. *Narcissism* was considered a normal condition for children during their early stages of development but was not expected to be found in mature adults. Currently, this is also called malignant **self-love** and is recognized as a means of self-protection used by those who have been severely traumatized at an early age. Because it is a feeling that attaches itself to others when the person feels admired, it can die and move on when gratification is no longer perceived.

Agape was recognized by Greek philosophers as the most radical kind of love because it was a **self-less** love. It referred to the love of Christians for others that corresponded to the love of God for mankind. It was defined as an unselfish love without sexual implications that esteemed others above self and was extended to all people, whether family members or distant strangers. *Agape* was later translated into Latin as *caritas*, which is the origin of our word *charity*. *Agape* is the most comprehensive description we have of who God is, and *God intended that mankind should mirror His kind of love.*

The next few paragraphs provide a partial list of attributes of God that people can mirror, the greatest being agape, *which proclaims that*

GOD is LOVE! (1 John 4:16) In other words, **GOD is AGAPE!** John 3:16 describes how deep His love is. Agape overshadows all types of human love. It means to love much, and when we view how God loves humanity, we see that agape is also a love that exists without any conditions. Agape does not die, and it does not change. It remains through every situation and covers everybody, whether a person is a believer, an agnostic, or an atheist. Agape is present for those who are murderers, sexual predators, pedophiles, thieves, liars, drug addicts, alcoholics, and those who practice any other type of sin. However, God's unconditional love for everybody does not mean that He accepts the sinful practices of mankind. God is love, but He is also holy, righteous, and just.

How important is agape? Agape is the reason God created people and a world that would sustain us. As beings created in the image and likeness of God, we are meant to express His love toward one another and His creation. People who claim to be Christians will not be viewed by the world as authentic unless God's love is on display through their words and deeds. Everything a believer says and does must be filtered through agape.

An understanding of what agape is and what it is not comes through learning Scripture and through personal experience with the Holy Spirit. Learning to practice agape is a life-long, ongoing process. As our temptation to sin decreases, and God's influence within increases, we are more and more able to reflect His loving nature.

There are several accounts of agape being extended to people who have been convicted of murder. Even though the pain from the loss of a loved one was still present, some relatives of the victim showed the love of God to the murderers by forgiving them. Several of the victim's survivors have even gone so far as to visit the murderer in prison and form a loving relationship. It is agape that enables a person to be forgiving in spite of the grief caused by losing a loved one through an act of violence.

GOD is HOLY. Although God's love covers all people, it is important to make a distinction between His love and His holiness. The best words I can use to describe holy are pure and blameless. God loves, but He does not condone willful sinning. Believers are commanded to stop our sinful practices and grow toward moral purity. As the influence of the love of God grows in a believer, His holy nature becomes more a part of who we are. The Apostle Paul wrote, "Because we have these promises, dear friends, let us cleanse ourselves from everything that can defile our body or spirit. And let us work toward complete holiness because we fear God" (2 Corinthians 7:1).

Growing in holiness is not something we do on our own. When we submit to God, He shows us our faults and how to change from our former, habitual ways of thinking and doing. The attribute of holiness gives a believer a sense of the difference between right and wrong and helps us choose to do what is right. God gave us rules of ethics to enable us to live with integrity. One aspect of integrity includes how we ethically relate to others. Another aspect of integrity concerns our inner person. Inner integrity is the state of being whole, entire, and undiminished. (*Dictionary.com Unabridged*) People are meant to have a healthy mind-set that results in honesty, transparency in speech, and moral character.

GOD is RIGHTEOUS. Righteousness has to do with our character. It is closely related to holiness, because holiness creates righteousness. A righteous character desires to do what is right according to what God says is right. When true holiness and righteousness are on display in a believer, and both are anchored in agape, the atmosphere all around a believer is changed, and others are blessed and encouraged.

GOD is MERCIFUL. Mercy is kind, sympathetic, and forgiving when dealing with someone who may be an offender, an enemy, or someone under the power of the one extending mercy. Believers learn to be merciful to others as we internalize the loving-kindness that God extended to us while we were still in a lost, sinful state prior to salvation.

GOD is BENEVOLENT. Benevolence is the desire to do good in ways that benefit others. God designed mankind to be interdependent and to work together as an organism rather than as an organization. He gave people the capacity and responsibility to benevolently relate to one another just as He benevolently relates to us. His benevolence is shown in the fact that it does not matter whether or not people love and honor Him, the earth continues to have the capacity to produce food and to supply water for the just and the unjust (see Matthew 5:45b).

GOD is CREATIVE. God created the world and everything in it out of nothing, and He gave mankind the ability to make things out of what He created. Mankind's creativity is seen in every area of life. To name a few, our creativity is seen in the areas of science, medicine, the arts, agriculture, technology, engineering, and manufacturing. Because of God's great love for His creation, whenever someone comes up with a creative idea, they should remember to give God thanks, because their idea was realized from what God had already made available to be discovered.

GOD is INTELLIGENT. He gave us wonderful brains with the ability to learn and the capacity for logical, sequential thought. We can intelligently communicate with one another through a variety of ways, such as through language, writing, the arts, and technology. Believers are called to have the mind of God, meaning that as we submit to transformation, we begin to use good judgment to make right decisions and choices that reflect His influence in our lives.

These various attributes of God are meant to work together in people to reflect His image. And it is extraordinary that every person is created in a way that we uniquely express His attributes. There has never been and never will be another person exactly like you. No matter how many people will be born, God created people who will never have an exact duplicate, not even among identical twins. When we fully grasp what it means to bear God's image, we are both awed by the possibilities of who we could be and saddened by the tragedy of our unrealized potential.

Until the sin problem is resolved in a person, the relationship with the One who created us remains broken, and it is impossible for people to obey God and be who He made us to be. But God's plan is that He came in the person of Jesus to open the way to a restored relationship and image. Don't rest until you can see God's image growing in you. It is only then that He can use you to draw others who desperately need to be in a relationship with Him.

Chapter 7
The Onion Example

Any branch in Me that does not bear fruit [that stops bearing] He cuts away (trims off, takes away); and He cleanses and repeatedly prunes every branch that continues to bear fruit, to make it bear more and richer and more excellent fruit. John 15:2 (AMP)

Once a person is saved, a life-long process of learning and growth begins. Believers are spoken of as branches that are part of a vine. The vine is understood to be the person of Jesus. The branches are expected to bear fruit.

But the Holy Spirit produces this kind of fruit in our lives: love, joy, peace, patience, kindness, goodness, faithfulness, gentleness, and self-control. There is no law against these things!
Galatians 5:22-23

Branches that don't bear fruit are cut off from the vine. The purpose of pruning the branches is to expose and correct that which is the most guarded in a person—the actual state of the heart. Jesus' concern is that a believer should see the true state of his or her heart and agree to the drastic change that is spoken of as transformation. The goal of pruning is a new heart that reflects God's Spirit.

Pruning can be loosely described by using the example of an onion that is formed with layers surrounding a core. In a believer, outer layers, or surface issues, are exposed, examined, and reshaped, where necessary. As the process goes deeper, a believer gains an honest insight into who he or she really is and of the need for change. The deeper the process is allowed to go, the more the state of the core, or the heart, is changed to reflect the image of God.

As mentioned before, when Jesus saves us, the Holy Spirit cleanses our spirits immediately. This work of God is miraculous and easy for Him. What follows is the hard part for a believer, because pruning affects the heart, which is where the temptation to disobey lies. Another name for pruning is *sanctification*, which means "to *make holy*." As a believer allows the sanctification process to deepen and reshape the mind and the desires of the will, the heart mirrors God more and more, and others can see the change.

The change is meant to be drastic, and it can be likened to the transformation of a caterpillar into a butterfly, where the butterfly looks nothing like the former caterpillar (Romans 12:2-3). Transforming a heart can be so difficult that many believers don't stay in the struggle, resulting in very little change after salvation. But if you as a believer will stick with it, your change can be so dramatic that people around you will see it and be drawn to the One who can do marvelous things.

Learning and internalizing Scripture, praying, and meditating are needed to change the heart and prepare it to participate with God.

> *Strip yourselves of your former nature [put off and discard your old unrenewed self] which characterized your previous manner of life and becomes corrupt through lusts and desires that spring from delusion; and be constantly renewed in the spirit of your mind [having a fresh mental and spiritual attitude], and put on the new nature (the regenerate self) created in God's image, [Godlike] in true righteousness and holiness.*
> *Ephesians 4:22-24 (AMP)*

Chapter 8
Consider the Fate of the Immortal Spirit

And he also said, "It is finished! I am the Alpha and the Omega—the Beginning and the End. To all who are thirsty I will give freely from the springs of the water of life. All who are victorious will inherit all these blessings, and I will be their God, and they will be my children. But cowards, unbelievers, the corrupt, murderers, the immoral, those who practice witchcraft, idol worshipers, and all liars—their fate is in the fiery lake of burning sulfur. This is the second death." Revelation 21:6-8

The bodies of human beings are animated, or given life, by our God-given, immortal spirits. One meaning of the word *immortal* is "unending life." Our immortal spirits will continue to live after our physical bodies die or are no longer needed. According to Scripture, the fate of those who die as unbelievers, without having been redeemed, is grim. Their fate is referenced in Revelation 21:8 and is the same fate as that of Satan, the beast, and the false prophet, stating that they will be tormented day and night forever and ever. (Revelation 20:10). Realizing this should encourage believers to seriously consider how to participate with God to provide heartfelt ministry to the unredeemed.

Satan opposes God and deceives people. He hates God, he hates the image of God in people, and he works relentlessly to corrupt all that is good. He aims to subvert any possibility of spiritual wholeness that is found only in relationship with God. He covets everyone's worship, so he is always working to keep people from experiencing the love and mercy of God. In general, people who don't submit to God continue to think they have power over their own lives to affect their future and destiny. Satan's evil influence works to hide from them the fact that their only real choice in life is who they will serve; either him or God. They don't realize that if they don't serve God, they either willingly or unknowingly serve the prince of this world.

Satan counterfeits himself as an "angel of light" and deceives those who are vulnerable (Ephesians 2:2). He relentlessly uses lies, tricks, and manipulation to lead people to disbelief in Jesus. He fights against people coming to know that Jesus is just who He said He is: the Savior of the World.

Those who become members of the Kingdom of God are saved from eternal damnation, and Satan loses the battle for their souls. But if he can divert the focus of believers away from the need for transformation, God's redemptive work in the world is hindered. It is unfortunate that many believers see the purpose of salvation only as a safety net to keep them out of hell. Once they are in what they believe to be the safety zone of salvation, they feel relieved and continue to live a shallow salvation experience. They miss the opportunity to be filled with the power of God and to walk the path that would lead them to the most wonderful life journey imaginable; a journey in submission to the God of unconditional love, growing and changing into entirely new people who help to draw others into a new life. When believers submit to transformation and learn how to participate with God, we become a spiritual force that draws people to Jesus and His saving power.

Take note! Everyone will live forever somewhere. What follows God's people after we die is eternal LIFE with our immortal spirits housed in a new, spiritual body that will never die. This is not promised to those who neglect God's gracious offer of salvation. Those who refuse a relationship with Him are promised a different eternal experience.

It is a myth that God *sends* people to hell. Unbelievers choose hell by refusing God. What follows them after they die is damnation, outside of God's life-giving, loving presence. Believers have a tremendous responsibility to focus on how God designed us so that we can effectively minister in His power and become beacons of light in this dark world.

Chapter 9
Does God Really See Me?

You saw me before I was born. Every day of my life was recorded in your book. Every moment was laid out before a single day had passed. How precious are your thoughts about me, O God. They cannot be numbered! Psalm 139:16-17

There are over 7 billion people in the world. You might ask, is God's love vast enough to cover every single person in the whole world? Considering all of those who are living now, does God really see *me*? The answers are YES, and YES! His love is abundant enough to include every person ever born until the end of time, and He is always aware of everyone.

It is incredible but true that God actually sees you all of the time and desires that you have a close relationship with Him! He knows your name and understands your needs. When you think of all the people who have ever lived and those who are yet to be born, how humbled are you that you have His attention right now?

God sent Jesus into the world to give people access to eternal life with Him. He did it knowing the hardship and cruelty that Jesus would face. He did it out of love (John 3:16).

There was a time when I was not aware of God; I didn't think about Him at all. But one day God opened my awareness and started me on a new path. I am continually amazed that out of the billions of people alive today, He saw me and my need for Him! Following are some of my personal experiences that made me know that God sees me.

One day I was sitting quietly, enjoying not having to do anything for a while. The room was unusually quiet and peaceful. Within that special atmosphere I heard a voice that said, "If you give up your grudge against your grandfather, you can be saved." Until then I didn't understand that my angry feelings against my grandfather were the same as a grudge. But when I heard those words, I immediately understood that this was true. To this day I am filled with wonder that I was able to so quickly respond by letting go of what was an unwarranted grudge.

My grandfather had done nothing more than tell me the truth about myself. Somehow I knew that the One who spoke to me and surrounded me with His presence was the Holy Spirit of God. How did I know? I believe that my spirit recognized the One from whom it came when I was conceived. I was surrounded by His presence. I surrendered and became His.

That day a second awesome thing happened. I had been trying to stop smoking for about two years. The presence of God gave me the power to stop that day. I actually threw away a half pack of cigarettes. Those of you who have been smokers know how serious that was. Those two experiences showed me how close we all are to the spiritual world, and that when God is ready, He will make His presence known.

Even though I had received forgiveness and welcomed God with my whole heart, I didn't attend a church right away. I rationalized that I spent most of my time working and taking care of my family. On Saturdays, I washed and cleaned and shopped. Sundays were when I rested in preparation for the next work week. But God made His presence known again.

About three weeks after I was saved, I had an experience at my workplace. This was many years ago, and I worked in the noisy environment of a keypunch facility. However, several people were off that day, and I once again found myself in an unusually quiet, peaceful atmosphere. I heard His still, small voice telling me why I should attend church services. He said, "You go to church because that is where believers gather together and strengthen one another." (That experience is why I love the word *believer*.) Once again I immediately accepted the truth of what I heard, and I abandoned my reasons for not attending church services. The following Sunday I joined a congregation.

Shortly after that, I had an angelic visitation. My husband worked nights, and one evening while I was alone in bed but still awake, my attention was drawn to an area across the room near the ceiling. Something was happening. It was like a door opening, and I heard the most beautiful, indescribable sound. It was like music, but more. I could not have identified an instrument, but the sound drew me in from the core of my being as my room was filled with it. Then I sensed two beings coming through the opening. One of them spoke only six words: "You are saved. You are free." After that they withdrew, the opening closed, the music was gone, and all was silent. To this day the memory of what I call heavenly music makes me long for the day when I will leave this world and go to the place where I can hear it again.

That night my awareness of God deepened, and I was reassured that I was saved. God prepared me ahead of time because He knew that soon an evil spirit would try to convince me that I was not saved. It happened a few weeks later while I was in my car on the way to an evening service. A voice spoke from behind me saying in a very emphatic, sarcastic, and cruel voice, "You are not saved!"

However, because of my previous experience, I was able to say without a shadow of a doubt, "Oh, yes, I am. I know it's true because the angel told me so."

Whoever spoke didn't respond, and I sensed that the presence was gone from my car.

Another experience happened years later when I was deeply hurt by someone close to me. I am an introvert, and the painful experience caused me to withdraw even more into myself. But one Sunday morning as I was listening to a sermon, something was said that made me realize that I had not only withdrawn from those around me, but I had also withdrawn from God. At that point I began to pray, asking God to forgive me. Then I heard His still, small voice whisper in such a loving way, "I understand."

Those two words spoke volumes to me. Even though I felt shame because I had not performed well, God let me know that

His love for me had not changed. His graciousness to me at that point was another pivotal moment in my relationship with Him. It helped me know Him and myself better. The experience taught me that I didn't need to perform. What I needed to do was have a deeper relationship with the One who loved me.

The point of this is to illustrate how spiritually healthy it is when we move past thinking only about the perishing part of John 3:16 that might cause us to believe we need to do certain things in order to be acceptable to God. Instead, we should concentrate on the phrase that states how much He loves us. Then we can move past needing to perform and focus on responding to His love in a way that will lead us to the rest and peace promised to those who love Him.

Verse 17 states that Jesus came not to judge, but to save. Judgment will come later, but for now, He loves us enough to look past our present shortcomings. He looks forward to what we can be if we submit and obey. Verse 16 mentions eternal life, which begins when Jesus saves us. When we transition into eternity, we are promised new, imperishable bodies and the ability to know God in a way that we cannot know Him in this material world. Every person born since the beginning is an immortal spirit housed in a human body. Those who trust in God will have eternal life with Him in a new, glorious body. Does God see you? Does God love you? You bet He does. And when you really come to know this, you will see the proof of His seeing and loving over and over again.

Chapter 10
Preparing to Participate with God

Now all glory to God, who is able, through his mighty power at work within us, to accomplish infinitely more than we might ask or think.
Ephesians 3:20

    Prerequisites for working with God are godly sorrow for sin, repentance, forgiveness, and salvation through accepting Jesus as Savior and Lord. Following that, you must submit to the rule of God in your life. Realizing how much He loves you will give you the desire to be entirely under His control. His power at work within you will enable you to rise above your selfish nature. Search for a version of the Bible that will make it easy for you to understand and internalize Scripture (see page 131 for suggestions). Learning Scripture will take a while, but continue to read and study.

    God has designed you for specific work. Learning how you

have been gifted to fulfill His calling on your life is discussed in Chapter 16.

As you take these necessary steps, God will lead you to your place in His service. As you internalize the Word of God and believe that He has the power to prepare you for service, He will lead you into your area of ministry. God will use His Holy Spirit, Scripture, godly teachers, and your life's experiences to train you for ministry.

People generally see life from the perspective of a worm's-eye view, which is a limited picture of life. Believers on the path of transformation take on the view of the eagle, which flies high and is able to see a much bigger picture. The bigger picture includes greater understanding of how God works and how you fit into His plan to help in the transformation of others.

People are meant to live in harmonious relationships. However, left to our own devices, we cannot create a lasting harmony in any area. No matter how hard we try or how much we care, we cannot stop the downhill slide of any good intention. If you take a look at history and current affairs, you will see the evidence of this. Year after year and century after century we see that left to ourselves, human beings are not capable of living together in peace or of pleasing God.

The evidence is the ongoing divisions and wars between nations, communities, and even among family members. What is at the root of divisions and wars? The spirits of evil at work in the world act in conjunction with the sinful nature of unredeemed people. Unfortunately, believers who do not submit to godly transformation are vulnerable to those spirits of division and disharmony.

God's plan enables people to rise above the negative influences in the world. His plan for you will come to fruition when you decide that, no matter what it takes, you will allow God to have His way in you. He came in the person of Jesus to help people like us become who we are meant to be. The Body of Christ is filled with those who are growing in the fruit of His indwelling Spirit, which is love, joy, peace, patience, kindness, goodness, faithfulness, gentleness, and self-control. Once you join with God, you will gain the ability and the privilege of being filled with His supernatural power. You will experience inner peace and joy, freedom from the constraints of fear, and an ability to radiate love and compassion that will draw others to Jesus through you.

God places high value on interpersonal relationships because as we lovingly live in dependence upon one another, a harmony is produced that builds people up. Living lives of godly love is the highest expression of who we are meant to be. Worldly love can divide people along the lines of bigotry, politics, tribal differences, gender, social or financial levels. Godly love unites, nourishes, and protects.

The Bible reminds us that the two most important areas of relating depend on agape (Mark 12:30-31). We must allow God to show us how to love Him with all that is in us, and when we love ourselves with His godly love, we can then love others in the same way. The transformation process can be quite a struggle, but God will lovingly and patiently instruct us as we walk with Him. He keeps His promises.

And I am certain that God, who began the good work within you, will continue his work until it is finally finished on the day when Christ Jesus returns.
Philippians 1:6

PART 3

What Are Believers Meant To Do?

He creates each of us by Christ Jesus to join him in the work he does, the good work he has gotten ready for us to do, work we had better be doing.
Ephesians 2:10c *(The Message)*

The biblical meaning of the word *good* relates to "that which is pleasing to God," or, "that which is valuable, virtuous, upright, and honorable in His sight." The biblical definition of good works does not stop at the good things we do for others. These good works encompass every aspect of our thinking and conduct in the sight of God. As we grow more and more pleasing to Him, His power enables us to be and do more than we could ask or think on our own. We are continually enticed to think bigger!

Chapter 11
A Change of Focus

Could it be any clearer? Our old way of life was nailed to the Cross with Christ, a decisive end to that sin-miserable life—no longer at sin's every beck and call! Romans 6:6 (The Message)

Part 2 discussed people in general, while this point forward focuses specifically on believers, from the perspective of the New Testament. First, in order to contrast people of the world who are under the rule of Satan with believers who are under the rule of God, I will provide some background. According to the Old Testament, the role of Adam and Eve was reasonably straightforward. While the earth and everything in it belong to God, He gave mankind some responsibilities, along with authority to govern the earth. They were to tend the earth, multiply and fill the earth, and govern the earth under His leadership. Only one commandment was given—they were not to eat from the tree of the knowledge of good and evil.

There came a time when Satan, in the form of a serpent, enticed Eve to eat the fruit from the forbidden tree. Her goal was to become all-knowing like God. Satan tricked Eve, who then influenced Adam, and they both sinned by disobeying God. In their effort to gain what they thought would make them equal to God in knowledge, they ended up with hardship and a loss of authority. Satan stole their God-given authority and became the ruler of this world. Adam and Eve were expelled from the garden, and from then on, all life was filled with trouble because of the influence of evil and its consistent interference in the lives of humankind.

Since the fall of Adam and Eve, the focus of what people are meant to do as it relates to participating with God is only on believers, because it is understood that the power of evil at work in the world makes it difficult for unbelievers to see and do what God desires.

God is not a tyrant like Satan. He gives people a choice of whom they will serve. This is called free will. Although God is ultimately responsible for what happens on earth, His choice to give people free will means that people cannot blame Him for the bad decisions they make or for the consequences of those decisions.

The New Testament refers to Satan as the "prince of the power of the air" and the "prince of demons" (Ephesians 2:2 (ESV), Luke 11:15). He is the root of the evil that works to ruin God's creation. Satan aims to steal, kill, and destroy all that is good. He works his evil strategies through people, and he wields great power through those who do not submit to God.

BUT, JESUS CAME! What hope is found in those three

words! Jesus came to show us who God is and open the way to a restored relationship through redemption and spiritual cleansing. Through His death and resurrection, Jesus broke the back of Satan's stranglehold and made a way of escape from the power of evil for all who will call upon His name (Romans 5:10 AMP). Believers have the power of the Holy Spirit dwelling within, which enables us to live right. Believers have access to what is called one of the most powerful forces on earth—the power of prayer. *The earnest prayer of a righteous person has great power and produces wonderful results. (James 5:16b)*

Because of Jesus, not only can believers overcome the power of evil in our own lives, but our prayers have the power to curtail and even prevent some of the evil activity in the world. God can equip believers to work with Him in a most marvelous way.

Chapter 12
It's All about Love

> *Watch what God does, and then you do it, like children who learn proper behavior from their parents. Mostly what God does is love you. Keep company with him and learn a life of love. Observe how Christ loved us. His love was not cautious but extravagant. He didn't love in order to get something from us but to give everything of himself to us. Love like that. Ephesians 5:1-2 (The Message)*

God really does work in mysterious ways. He began to draw me before I was saved and before I knew anything about Him or about love. My first experience with God and His love was through a dream initiated by Him. In the dream I was standing somewhere alone. As I became more aware of my surroundings, I noticed that I was encircled by a narrow ring of what looked like a cloudy substance. As I focused on this substance, it expanded into three distinct horizontal forms that were still joined by the ring.

(It was seeing the three forms joined together that helped me to understand the three persons of God after I was saved.)

As I stood there, I began to feel a strong force emanating from the three forms. I was made to understand that this force was love. The effect of it was empowering and strengthening because it was full of acceptance and caring. His outpouring of love was more than I had ever experienced from a person. Because this happened before I was saved, you might ask how I knew this was God. I can only say that when you have an encounter with God, there is no room for confusion. He makes Himself known.

Later, after Jesus saved me and I remembered the dream, the memory of it worked along with other experiences that changed how I perceived myself. I learned that I have value, that I am lovable, and that my life has meaning. I was humbled by knowing that Jesus gave His life for ordinary people like me. I experienced how the love of God can build up and strengthen people, no matter who we are or what we have done in the past.

GOD is LOVE! His plan for mankind and the world is all about LOVE. Every attribute that He shares with mankind is an expression of His love. As believers, we are meant to imitate God by being expressions of His love in this world. Believers are God's new creations, spiritually reborn after having been designed in advance to work with Him (Ephesians 2:10).

Jesus' love is extravagant. He came to serve, not to be served. In order to work in ways that will enrich the lives of others, a believer must imitate Jesus and live a life of sacrificial service. Every believer has a ministry. Our work encompasses both the Body of Christ and the world. The Body of Christ is designed to be interdependent, and believers are meant to work together to make the Body of Christ healthy and strong by using our God-given talents, skills, abilities, and gifts, as the Holy Spirit directs. The other area of our service is as God's ambassadors who shine His light into a dark world.

Serving sometimes presents relational difficulties. During those times, agape, or godly love, must be on display. *Love* is always an interesting word, because it means different things to different people, as was stated in Chapter 6. Loving like God is a conscious choice we can make. It is a matter of principle and duty, and it continues even through difficult struggles. The presence of God's superabundant love in believers gives us the ability to love anybody, and we are not constrained in how much love we should or can give. Agape is not bigoted, and it does not condemn or hate people. It does not get offended and sink to the level of unforgiveness or bitterness. It recognizes evil, but it is not overcome by evil. Agape is respectful, even in the face of evil. Notice the example of respect the archangel Michael showed toward Satan, the prince of evil, as he contended for Moses' body:

> *But even Michael, one of the mightiest of the angels, did not dare accuse the devil of blasphemy, but simply said, "The Lord rebuke you!" Jude 1:9*

Instead of treating Satan with arrogance or condemnation, Michael left judgment in the hands of God, as He is the only one who can judge any of us, including Satan himself.

Consider what can happen when *human* love is displeased or offended. What do people normally do when someone offends them? Common responses are to feel hurt, get angry, treat the other with disdain, or even worse, seek revenge and practice some type of cruelty to get even or punish the offender.

Notice how Peter tells us to respond:

> *For God called you to do good, even if it means suffering, just as Christ suffered for you. He is your example, and you must follow in his steps. He never sinned, nor ever deceived anyone. He did not retaliate when he was insulted, nor threaten revenge when he suffered. He left his case in the hands of God, who always judges fairly. 1 Peter 2:21-23*

Jesus was scoffed at, humiliated, and even physically tortured during His ministry on earth. In those times of suffering, he looked beyond Himself and honored God. He didn't complain or argue. He didn't retaliate or threaten revenge. He didn't fight verbally or physically, although He could have—at any moment—EASILY dealt harshly with anyone he wished. He wasn't like us—he didn't have to endure torture or death by crucifixion because he was not physically trapped as we mere mortals would be. He chose God's way. He could have freed himself from His suffering at any time, but chose not to, because He was determined to complete God's plan for us.

There was an incident when Jesus reacted out of anger that may appear to have been a contradiction to Peter's teaching. One day in the temple, Jesus used a whip on the money changers and overturned their tables (John 2:13-17). On the face of it, this may look like an act of violence because Jesus felt personally offended. However, there is no contradiction here, because Jesus' anger was not personal. It was based on the abominable acts being practiced in His Father's house. His passion for God's house brought that response. And since He was God in the flesh, He had authority to do what He did. There are two lessons here for us.

First, we must be careful that we don't react in a negative way when we feel personally offended. Reacting in anger to personal offenses is self-righteous anger. Second, if we do experience truly righteous anger as Jesus did in the temple, we must be careful that we don't take God's place and overstep our authority. We must be careful to discern God's will before we overtly react to things that He considers abominable. Rather, we must always seek to be led by God and honor Him in our actions and attitudes. Jesus' priority was to be a humble and obedient servant of God. He is our example in all things.

Chapter 13
Every Believer Has a Specific Calling

The Word of God speaks eloquently to His purpose and calling on our lives:

Romans 8:28
And we know that God causes everything to work together for the good of those who love God and are called according to his purpose for them.

Romans 1:1 (NIV)
*Paul, a servant of Christ Jesus, **called** to be an apostle and set apart for the gospel of God—*

Ephesians 4:7
*However, he has given each one of us a **special gift** through the generosity of Christ.*

Romans 12:6 (AMP)
*Having **gifts** (faculties, talents, qualities) that differ according to the grace given us, let us use them...*

Ephesians 2:10c (The Message)
*He creates each of us by Christ Jesus to join him in the work he does, the **good work** he has gotten ready for us to do, work we had better be doing.*

The word *gifts* in this context is translated from the Greek word *charisma*, which are spiritual endowments, also called spiritual anointings.

We tend to give the words *purpose* and *calling* the same meaning. However, in the context of God's gifts, it is helpful to view the two words from different levels. Our purpose, as a command of God, is to love and serve Him first, and then to love and serve others (Mark 12:30-31). Purpose, then, is best seen from the eagle's eye view where we see the big picture of **who** we are to serve.

Because the design of each individual is unique and personal, a *calling* is best seen from the worm's-eye view, which gives a detailed picture of **how** and **where** we are to serve. Every believer is designed for a unique ministry. Contrary to how many have viewed the work of pastors as those who do the bulk of the work of ministry, the Bible tells us that their work is to help train the members to do the work of ministry (Ephesians 4:11-12).

When a person submits to God and is redeemed, God makes His calling known to all who will hear. As a believer, your calling can be described as *a "strong inner impulse toward a particular course of action, especially when accompanied by a conviction of divine influence"* (Merriam-Webster Dictionary). *Your calling is spiritually directed and based on your unique design. Your calling is related to the things you are passionate about and good at because of your unique talents, skills, and abilities, and the gifts you receive after you are saved. Your design first points to* **where** *you should serve.*

God is consistent in His plan for each of our lives. He would not give us inborn talents, skills, abilities, temperaments, spiritual gifts, and various life experiences, and then not want us to use them! Imagine giving a loved one a wonderful gift, hoping she will not throw it in the trash or lose it forever in a closet, never to be taken out of the box! God dearly wants us to recognize and use the gifts He gave us.

Broadly speaking, your area of service can be recognized by two factors, FRUITFULNESS and FULFILLMENT. Perhaps you have noticed those times when you served others in some capacity where they were blessed and enlightened by what you said or did, *and* you experienced a strong sense of satisfaction. If your service was fruitful, and you experienced fulfillment, you were probably working in the area of your godly design. This is the area on which you should focus.

Your place of service may be different from that of others with the same calling. Therefore, it is necessary to find **how** God has fitted you to serve. For example, someone with the gift of teaching may not be designed to work with all age groups or genders. I have the gift of teaching, but I learned early on that I have not been designed to work with children or teenagers, with those in their formative years. I am called to work with adults who have a yearning to learn more about what God has for them. You will be most fruitful and fulfilled when you find your place of service.

Here is another example. There is a difference of focus for the gifts of evangelist and pastor. Someone with the gift of evangelism generally focuses on unbelievers, interacting with people outside of the church walls who are in need of salvation. Someone with the gift of pastor focuses on believers within the church walls and oversees those who are already saved. Even though the two roles may sometimes overlap, their areas of service are specific to their gifts.

Your calling may be carried out in a local or regional ministry, or, like Billy Graham, you may have a worldwide calling. An important thing to remember is that your calling is not your decision. It was decided by God before you were born. It was His choice as to how you are designed. Answering the call on your life is how you work with God. You will function most effectively when you recognize your calling and then work wherever God desires to place you.

Chapter 14
Gifted to Serve Others

He makes the whole body fit together perfectly. As each part does its own special work, it helps the other parts grow, so that the whole body is healthy and growing and full of love. Ephesians 4:16

References to gifts in the Bible are found in Romans 12:6-8; Ephesians 4:8, 11-12; Hebrews 2:4; and 1 Peter 4:10-11. The most thorough teaching on gifts is found in 1 Corinthians 12. In verse 7, Paul explains one of the benefits of gifts, which is to enhance the Body of Christ:

But to each one is given the manifestation of the [Holy] Spirit [the evidence, the spiritual illumination of the Spirit] for good and profit. (AMP)

God desires to work supernaturally through believers. The need for you to fulfill your unique calling in the Body of Christ is imperative, and your service will become increasingly effective if you are in the process of transformation (Romans 12:1-2).

Learning to think like God is what makes it possible for us to continue to live in this world and not be part of its way of living. Consider, for example, how this world trains people to perform rather than be authentic. We live in a world where we are taught and conditioned to believe that we are given what others decide we deserve. For example, if we perform well in school, we get good grades. If we fail to perform well, we get bad grades and may be treated as failures. The problem with failure could be that what was offered in the classroom didn't meet needs. Or, if we meet expectations on our jobs, we are eligible for raises. Otherwise, our salaries won't increase, and we might even be fired.

If we look good to others, perform well in the minds of others, and please people, we can gain various levels of acceptance and make progress in a social hierarchy. Otherwise, we might be ignored, devalued, and held back.

After a salvation experience, we may carry that same mindset and apply it to God, thinking that God requires us to perform for Him in order to be rewarded with His good will and blessings. I had that mindset. I was performance oriented and needed to stay busy doing what I considered to be godly activities. I didn't realize that in my effort to perform, I was always in fear of what God or people would think if I failed to perform well in their eyes. My thinking was wrong. I don't have to fear people, because what people think is secondary to God's thoughts about me. I was wrong to think I needed to earn God's love and good will. I always, already had that. We all do.

My error was also in thinking that my performance, or my actions, were the same as giving good service to God. I learned to ask valuable questions of myself: Is what I am doing accomplishing what God wants? What is His purpose and calling for me? How can I please Him and in turn, truly bless others? On introspection, I saw that trying to do things by using my human reasoning was not pleasing to Him or productive for me. Trying to please God by doing things out of a sense of duty and fear is a waste of precious time. Performing self-reasoned acts fell far short of the freedom and joy that were promised to me. My intentions seemed good, but my actions missed the mark. I needed to learn what God wants me to do.

I began to meditate to learn what to do to please Him. In the process, I experienced another shift in my perspective. I finally understood that because He already loves me, it is a waste of time to try to earn His love and acceptance. No manner of performance is needed. A relationship that brings knowledge and understanding is what is needed. The way to please God is spelled out by Jesus:

> *Are you tired? Worn out? Burned out on religion? Come to me. Get away with me and you'll recover your life. I'll show you how to take a real rest. Walk with me and work with me—watch how I do it. Learn the unforced rhythms of grace. I won't lay anything heavy or ill-fitting on you. Keep company with me and you'll learn to live freely and lightly. Matthew 11:28-30 (The Message)*

The salvation experience through Jesus opens the possibility of a deep relationship with God. However, a believer does not change much if his relationship with God remains shallow. Unfortunately, not all believers see the need for transformation, so they fail to learn what God wants from them or how to please Him. If you have not allowed your relationship to deepen, you may not recognize the calling for which you were born. And even if you recognize it, you may not be drawn into it.

One evening during a worship service, I had a vision. God showed me a pew at the front of the church where several men and women were seated. He told me that each of them had been given the call to preach His word, and though all had understood their call, not one of them had answered it. How sad it is that the wonderful gifts bestowed upon believers are often left unused. When we don't fill our place in ministry, the love of God is cut off from someone who needs what we were designed to give.

If you are a believer and are not serving others through your calling, you are living beneath your privilege of being filled with the joy and peace and satisfaction that come from knowing God is pleased with your obedience and productive service.

As my perspective on performance shifted, I could see that He gets pleasure from watching me be transformed as my thinking processes change. He is pleased with me as I grow to become who He meant for me to be and doing what He means for me to do, which is to answer the call for which I was designed. When I worship Him, we are both pleased.

He is pleased when I submit to His will instead of to my own. He loves it when I relate lovingly to others. His pleasure stems from the fact that through His power I am less and less under the influence of my human nature and more and more under the influence of His divine nature. Jesus loved extravagantly and served others rather than Himself. He is our example!

Chapter 15
You Are Unique

> *God's various expressions of power are in action everywhere; but God himself is behind it all. Each person is given something to do that shows who God is: . . . All kinds of things are handed out by the Spirit, and to all kinds of people!*
> 1 Corinthians 12:6-7 (The Message)

Understanding your unique design requires time, meditation, and study. Gift discovery is an important ministry for a local church that can help believers learn their calling and find their place of service. Perhaps your church already has an in-depth gift discovery program. If not, I recommend the book, <u>Discover Your Spiritual Gifts</u>, by C. Peter Wagner. His book can help you recognize your gifts and how to use them. It includes the Wagner-Modified Houts Questionnaire, which is a series of questions and additional information that will help you know yourself better. Answering the questions should point to what are your top three

Spiritual gifts. You can also search several websites that can help you discover how you are gifted. One of those is mintools.com/spiritual-gifts.htm. Are you getting excited about discovering how God has designed you?

Here is a good reason why you should be excited. The joy of doing what you were made to do far outweighs the mundane tasks you may occasionally take on that give you no real joy or long-term sense of fulfillment. I know many believers who thought it was their duty to help out wherever there was a need. It didn't seem to matter if they enjoyed the task or if they felt any excitement as they served because their sense of duty made them think they were doing a good thing regardless of the task, who is served or if it blessed those being served. They used their own or someone else's reasoning to decide where they should serve.

I agree that it is good to temporarily meet an immediate need that is outside of your calling. But I encourage you to focus on the specific work for which you were designed. What a different impact churches would have if members were taught to use God's wisdom and insight about how they should serve. If believers let God lead them to their calling, the dynamics of serving would become joyful and productive to both the server and those being served.

The Apostle Paul knew that when members served one another through their gifts, the Body of Believers grew healthy, every need was met, and the love of God could be seen by all, both in the local church and outside of the church. Every need included the:

- Physical for clothing, shelter, and food
- Mental for mutual encouragement to grow in sound thinking
- Spiritual for growth in godliness

He makes the whole body fit together perfectly. As each part does its own special work, it helps the other parts grow, so that the whole body is healthy and growing and full of love. Ephesians 4:16

As God's ambassadors, believers are needed as lights that shine in the darkness of the world, reflecting His loving, spiritual, benevolent, creative, intelligent, communicative, relational, ethical, and moral characteristics. Serving through your calling is the path to your greatest fulfillment and the rich blessing of others. You will feel the greatest pleasure and wholeness when who God made you to be is being developed and expressed by doing what He intends for you to do.

God's plan is ingenious. Although you received some traits from your parents, you were also given traits that are uniquely your own. You have a set of unique talents, skills, and abilities. And you have other things that are uniquely yours such as your personality, level of intelligence, ethnicity, gender, and even your physical shape. Where you were born is not an accident. Nothing in your design was by chance. And God has placed within you passions about certain things that are meant to lead you to your calling.

All that you obtained before birth, and afterward from your life's experiences, are meant to be used by God in specific ways for the blessing of people and our physical world. When you received Jesus as Savior, the anointing of God became available to help you work for good in ways you could not accomplish on your own.

God gives each of us what He wants us to have and then helps us understand how to live a purpose-filled life His way, which is the best way. Nobody is great at everything. We all have strengths and weaknesses. God made us to complement one another. Where we are strong we can support others where they are weak, and vice-versa. No matter how independent we might wish to be, we need to work together.

Only you can fill your place. Learning and developing your calling can be scary, but it is worth pushing your fear aside and trusting God's wisdom. After all, He is the one who made you! As your trust deepens, you will begin to rejoice as you learn how much God values you as a unique individual, and your life will take on a new character and direction. Your self-image will take on a balance that rules out arrogance as you realize you cannot mature in godliness on your own. You will begin to look forward to doing what God wants to do through you.

Most believers will not serve as paid employees of a church ministry, so there is an added benefit for those who are able to earn a living in a secular job that coincides with their calling. This can make their everyday work an enjoyable and exciting experience. Those who need to earn a living doing work that does not match their calling may have a boring job-related experience. But there is even an upside to that if they are able to minister in the area of their calling outside of their secular job.

Chapter 16
How to Recognize Your Design

I could not stop thanking God for you—every time I prayed, I'd think of you and give thanks. But I do more than thank. I ask—ask the God of our Master, Jesus Christ, the God of glory—to make you intelligent and discerning in knowing him personally, your eyes focused and clear, so that you can see exactly what it is he is calling you to do, grasp the immensity of this glorious way of life he has for Christians, oh, the utter extravagance of his work in us who trust him —endless energy, boundless strength! Ephesians 1:16-19 (The Message)

An understanding of your design will increase as your personal relationship with God deepens, and as you get to know yourself better. Taking time to assess who you really are is of great value. For a while, I facilitated a personality assessment as part of a gift discovery course. Class members learned that they didn't know themselves as well as they had thought because they took so much of who they are for granted. The personality assessment asked questions that made them think deeply about things they hadn't paid much attention to.

Following is a system that will help you see yourself more clearly. It will help you learn how you are spiritually gifted and how to focus on those things about which you are passionate. It will highlight your personality type and the way in which your experiences have impacted you. The system uses the SHAPE acronym, which stands for Spiritual Gifts, Heart, Abilities, Personality, and Experiences. When taken as a whole, these five factors will help to clarify your design. Go through the following steps in the order of your choosing.

1. Discover your **SPIRITUAL GIFTS** by taking advantage of the information given at the beginning of Chapter 15.
2. Focus on the motivations of your **HEART** by thinking about what you love to do. God implanted certain passions as part of your design. The hardships of life may have caused you to ignore those things that you loved to do as a child. If so, think back and pull those things to the front of your memory. When you do this, you should feel a rekindling of your lost passion. Physiologically, each of us has a unique heartbeat with a pattern that is slightly different from anyone else's. Likewise, God has given

each of us a unique emotional heartbeat that will race when we encounter activities, subjects, or circumstances that keenly interest us. We instinctively feel deeply about some things and care little about others. Your emotional heartbeat points to what your interests are and what brings you the greatest sense of fulfillment. It motivates you to pursue certain activities, subjects, and environments. Make a list of those things that you loved to do as a child and as an adult.

3. It has been said that the average person has between five hundred and seven hundred **ABILITIES**, most of which we take for granted. Think about those things you do well that come naturally. There are a number of skills that seem to be inborn, or were developed in your early years. When people say, "You just seem to have a natural talent for it," it's probably true! People who play sports well have certain skills that preclude others from participating at the same high level because they lack the needed skills. People who love to build things have special skills and abilities. They can envision a finished product before the building has begun. Those who are drawn to being caregivers, such as doctors and nurses, have yet another set of special skills and insights. Make a list of your accomplishments from childhood to the present. Circle all **verbs** that denote **actions performed** as you were achieving your goal. Try to be specific. Take notice of which are your strongest. There are no unspiritual abilities. God gave them, and all can be useful in His service.

4. Consider your **PERSONALITY**. This factor is very important in matching you to the right ministry, because how you relate to others is a key to finding where you are best fitted to serve. For example, extroverts and introverts may fit into the same area of service, but in different ways. Unless you have taken time to assess your personality, you probably don't know yourself as well as you think you do. God does not use a cookie cutter to stamp out people uniformly. He has wired your temperament in a unique way, because He loves variety—just look around! And there is no right or wrong personality type. We need variety to balance the church. A personality assessment will help you understand how you interact with others. If you have not completed a personality assessment, I recommend *Personality Types: Using the Enneagram for Self-Discovery,* by Don Richard Riso and Russ Hudson. For now, consider using the following exercise that will point to some personality traits you have and may draw you into further investigation:

Where do you get your energy?
- **Extroverts** get their energy from interacting with others. When they are alone, they lose energy. In order to get re-energized, they must get back to interacting with others.
- **Introverts** lose energy from interacting with others and need to spend time alone to re-energize.

Which process do you use to make decisions?
- **Thinkers** take time to think things through before making decisions.
- **Feelers** make decisions based on their feelings.

In which environment are you most comfortable?
- The most comfortable lifestyle for some is having **Routine** schedules.
- The most comfortable lifestyle for others is one that is full of **Variety**.

How do you react?
- Those who are **Self-controlled** think before they act.
- Those who are **Self-expressive** act without much prior thought.

Do you enjoy following or leading?
- Those who enjoy following are called **Cooperative**.
- Those who enjoy leading are called **Competitive.**

5. Consider your various **EXPERIENCES**. Life has taught you some things through your many ups and downs. Think about how your **painful** experiences have shaped your life. Consider your **educational** experiences and those subjects that were most interesting. If you have had **ministry** experiences, focus on those that blessed others and gave you a strong sense of fulfillment.

I love the concept of the motivations of our hearts because they are strong indicators of our God-given callings. The things we love to do can work in us like the proverbial bread crumbs that lead a hungry animal to food. What was it that you loved to do in your early years? Did you love to sing, or dance, or write; to build or grow things; or learn the science of things? Did you dream of becoming a doctor or a nurse, or a teacher?

God can use your love for designing and developing and making something out of what seems to be nothing. Or, He can use your love for pioneering and venturing into new areas. You may be someone who loves to organize and bring order out of chaos. If you love to assist others in their responsibilities, you are one who helps others succeed. Perhaps you love to excel, to be the best at what you do, and attain the highest standards. If you love to shape attitudes and behaviors of others, you are probably a natural mentor. Perhaps you love to prevail and fight for what is right, opposing what is wrong, because you love to overcome injustice. Did you love to make money?

There is some confusion surrounding the subject of money. A misunderstanding of Scripture has led some to think that money itself is the root of all evil. However, the Bible tells us that the root of all evil is the *love* of money (1 Timothy 6:10). Jesus warned people that they could not serve both God and money (Matthew 6:24).

The way a person deals with the subject of money points to the state of his heart. Jesus exposed the motive behind the love of money as greed for wealth, which is the sin of avarice. But, if the heart is right and puts God first, loving to make money is not a sin, nor is having an abundance of money a sin. A love for generating funds that is grounded in the right motive can be a great blessing, because money is needed to finance ministry. Using an inborn, God-given talent for making money used in His service honors God.

Some motivations or passions may not sound spiritual. For example, I heard a story about a newly saved man who was motivated to start a backpacking ministry at his church. If that activity does not seem to be spiritual, consider the outcome of his ministry. He and others like him loved to study the Bible in an outdoor, natural setting where they read, prayed, and encouraged one another to have a close relationship with God. God's design in people can produce ministries that will satisfy every need.

Your brain is a marvelous organ. Your God-given passions and dreams were implanted there, waiting for you to realize them. Think about how God has designed you to express what you love to do through your natural talents, skills, and abilities. Once He anoints all that He planted within you, He can marvelously use you to bless not only the Body of Christ, but also unbelievers within your sphere of influence.

Coming to understand your design is not rocket science. You can learn your SHAPE as you prayerfully apply yourself toward understanding what God has done in you. How much bigger should you be thinking? How much more can you open up to God's plan for you? Once you discover your calling, you can take to the skies like the eagle and see the bigger picture. You can soar to new heights with God! Here is a quote from Pastor Rick Warren's gift discovery material:

*"My ministry will be most effective and fulfilling when I am using my **GIFTS** and **ABILITIES** in the area of my **HEART'S DESIRE** in a way that best expresses my **PERSONALITY** and **EXPERIENCE**."*

Be determined *to learn what His plan is for you.*
Be resolved *that neither your own feelings, nor those of other people, nor the devil, will stop you from entering into God's plan for your life.*

Chapter 17
Some Gift Examples

Following are examples of five people who are joyfully participating with God by living out His calling on their lives.

Dan, the Pastor

Dan has the gift of Pastor. His gift gives him the special ability to spiritually care for, protect, guide, and feed a group of believers entrusted to his care.

Literal Meaning of Pastor: *to shepherd or oversee.* This gift includes various areas of responsibility and is closely related to the gift of leadership.

Pastor Dan also has the gift of Teaching, which is the special ability to instruct others in the Bible in a logical, systematic way to communicate pertinent information for true understanding and growth.

Literal Meaning of Teaching: *To instruct.*

People with this gift mix of Pastor/Teacher:

- Put the Word of God at the center of their lives
- Care for the spiritual well-being of a local body of God's people
- Prepare through extended times of study and reflection
- Present the whole counsel of God for maximum life change
- Teach the Word of God, giving attention to detail and accuracy

References: Jeremiah 3:15, Acts 20:28, Romans 12:7b, 1 Corinthians 12:28, Ephesians 4:11, 2 Timothy 2:2

Pastor Dan's heart is that of a servant who does not require fame or recognition for himself and gratefully welcomes God's grace on his life. In the exercise of his gifts, he leads with thoughtfulness and compassionate understanding; he is slow to speak and quick to love. He probes Scripture and explains it in a way that makes it relevant and easy to understand by using modern-day examples and situations.

****

Leon, the Evangelist

Leon has the gift of Evangelism, which is the special ability to be a messenger of the good news of the Gospel in a way that draws unbelievers into the Body of Christ.

Literal Meaning of Evangelize: *To bring good news.*

People with this gift:

- Communicate the message of the Bible with clarity and

conviction
- Seek out opportunities to talk to unbelievers about spiritual matters
- Can insert spiritual truths into normal conversation with unsaved people, and can sense the timing of when to do so
- Challenge unbelievers to faith and to become fully devoted followers of Jesus
- Adapt the presentation of the gospel to connect with the individual's needs
- Have the ability to converse easily with strangers and people of short acquaintance
- Seek opportunities to build relationships with unbelievers

References: Ephesians 4:11, Acts 8:26-40

Leon's heart is fixed on the redemption of others. He does not see people as strangers, but rather as those who God wants to redeem. He is able to engage people in any venue, such as a bowling alley, a grocery store checkout, waiting in line at a movie theater, or at a car wash. His manner of addressing others is not judgmental or condescending. His anointing draws people to listen as he speaks.

****

Carmella, the Helper

Carmella has the gift of Helps, which is the special ability to render support or assistance to others in the Body to free them up for ministry, giving practical support for necessary tasks.

Literal Meaning of Help: *To take the place of someone.*

People with this gift:
- Serve behind the scenes wherever needed to support the gifts and ministries of others
- See the tangible and practical things to be done and enjoy doing them
- Sense God's purpose and pleasure in meeting everyday responsibilities
- Attach spiritual value to practical service
- Enjoy knowing that they are freeing up others to do what God has called them to do

References: 1 Corinthians 12:28, Romans 16:1-2

Carmella serves with patience and joy. When she learns what kind of help is needed, she gets busy deciding the best approach to get the job done. She has all of the traits listed above, and people love to have her on their team.

****

Teresa, the Servant

Teresa has an awesome gift of Service, which is the special ability to identify undone tasks in God's work, however menial, and use available resources to get the job done.

Literal Meaning of Service: *any act of service done in genuine love for the edification of the community.*

People with this gift:
- Can be adept at financing, planning, organizing, delegat-

ing responsibilities and problem-solving; are task oriented and organize things, events, or programs with excellence
- Could also be good leaders who emphasize personal relationship and leadership responsibilities
- Are concerned with details and organization
- Are determined to bring plans to completion

References: Acts 6:1-7, Romans 12:7, 1 Corinthians 16:15-16, Hebrews 13:1-2, 1 Peter 4:9

Teresa's serving ability is enhanced by her organizational skill. Her tenacious, pit-bull determination to get things done makes her a force to be reckoned with. Once she gets started on a project, she does not quit until a problem is fixed, a dilemma is resolved, and the task is completed. The force of her personality is tempered by the power of the love of God on display in her. These two characteristics make one happy to just stand back and watch her work. She has a secondary gift of Hospitality. She deeply cares about the well-being of others and will work tirelessly to ensure that the physical needs of others are met.

****

Michelle, the Exhorter

Michelle has the gift of Exhortation, sometimes called the gift of counseling, which is the special ability to come alongside someone with words of encouragement, comfort, consolation, and counsel to help them be all God wants them to be.

Literal Meaning of Exhort: *To encourage.*

People with this gift:
- Listen carefully to others to know the appropriate words that encourage
- Are able to discern unspoken needs
- Hear the Holy Spirit as He enlightens them in what is right
- Act correctly in times of trials and troubles
- Are able to remain balanced to offer right counsel and understanding to others

References: Isaiah 11:2-3, Acts 14:21-22, Romans 12:8a

Time after time I have noticed how Michelle conducted herself in the face of suffering, either her own or that of others. She remained calm and patient and was able to offer consolation to others in their suffering. She has traits that make for an excellent spiritual counselor because she is able to speak God's truth into life's circumstances.

****

I could have included many other godly men and women who have recognized their gifts, their place in ministry, and who are serving with their whole hearts. A list of gift descriptions can be found in the Appendix.

My friend, always remember this: You really can be who God said you can Be, AND You really can do what God said you can Do!

PART 4

Your Calling Is Already Yours!

CLAIM IT!

For we are God's masterpiece. He has created us anew in Christ Jesus so we can do the good things he planned for us long ago. Ephesians 2:10

Chapter 18
Does Your Perspective Need to Change?

At this point, does the idea that you have a calling still intimidate you? Remember, that if Jesus has saved you, the Bible says:

You are His masterpiece, created anew to be used by Him.
God has designed you for your calling.
It is His job to train you in how to work with Him.

These three things are all works of God. Your part is to believe Him and submit. Allow Him to have His way in you. He knows who you can be in spite of who you may be now. Be careful that you don't maintain an attitude of unbelief about who you can be and what God can do. We read in the Bible about the miraculous things God did in the past, but we can be skeptical about what He will do in the present, or with us. This is unbelief at work.

Jesus said that anything is possible if a person believes (Mark 9:23). He was talking to a father who asked Jesus to help *if* He could. (Of course, He can.) Deeper trust is called for if you are a believer but still have some areas of unbelief. If so, you might find it easier to believe what you cannot do than to believe God and get involved in the work. If you are still in doubt, your perspective needs to change.

God understands your propensity to doubt based on some bad experiences from your past. However, He wants to use those experiences to help you grow in wisdom. It has been said that God doesn't waste life's hurtful experiences. He can take *any* bad experience and make it work for good. In order to take on a believing-God perspective, pray and ask Him to help you in your unbelief so that your ability to believe will broaden. There is no greater or surer way to grow in your faith than to pray to God for a closer connection with Him.

Prayer and Bible study are two keys to thinking bigger about God. But those won't work until you decide to trust what you learn. God does not change. He is the same yesterday, today, and forever. He loves you. He values you, and He wants to have a deep relationship with you. Begin to view yourself in the same way King David viewed himself. He wrote,

> *Thank you for making me so wonderfully complex!*
> *Your workmanship is marvelous—how well I know it.*
> *Psalm 139:14*

This is not arrogance. It is recognizing that God values you. Continue to tell yourself that it is God alone who defines who you are. As you repeat this day after day, the thought will soon take root in your mind and what you believe about yourself will change. You will take on God's view of who you are. Thinking bigger is not about what you can do on your own. It is about believing what you can do through His power at work in you.

I wonder how Billy Graham felt when he accepted that his gift was evangelism on a wide scale? How did he overcome his own doubts and forge ahead in a way that touched millions of people over the course of many years? He must have come to firmly believe that God was leading him. He moved into thinking bigger about God as his trust deepened. Faith is believing what God says. Believing what God says is a result of allowing the Spirit to renew your thoughts and attitudes (Ephesians 4:23).

Take courage. God didn't give you a spirit of fear (2 Timothy 1:7). Fear is a learned mindset. Fear is of this world. It didn't come from God, but it can be conquered through Him. Believe me, you can do it!

Chapter 19
Love Yourself

...You shall love your neighbor as [you do] yourself. Matthew 19:19b (AMP)

What is your perspective on yourself? Do you really love yourself? The Greek word for loving others in this verse is *agapao*, which means to have much love for others. But before we can properly love others, we must have a proper love for ourselves. Think back to the list of the various expressions of love in Chapter 6. Agape is the highest because it is a godly love. This is how we must come to love ourselves. We are all products of our environment, and we express what we have learned.

From a very young age, I lived with criticism, fault-finding, and condemnation. That experience gave me a negative opinion of myself. I mirrored how I had been treated. But later, as the Word of God and the indwelling Holy Spirit began to have an impact, I learned that how I viewed myself needed to change. I saw that I didn't know what love is and that I didn't love myself.

But, thank God, I have learned to view myself objectively and not attach negative emotions to what I see. I try to understand what prompts an action and the motive behind it. If I decide that something in me needs to change, I pray to God for His perspective about the matter, because I want to see myself through His eyes. In the process, I get to know myself better. I practice the same mercy with myself that I am expected to practice with others. Without making excuses, I understand that some changes are more difficult than others, and I allow the transforming process to continue. My expectation is that where I need to grow in understanding and wisdom, God will provide both if I remain open to Him.

One day long ago, God accepted me into His kingdom just as I was. Because He treated me with tender mercy and grace, I am determined to extend the same to others. And even if I don't like what I see in others, God is the judge, not me. My goal is to love like God. We have all traveled a path that began somewhere long ago. But as we allow God to change our thinking, we can create new paths and new perspectives.

The Holy Spirit gave me a big boost one day while I wrestled with a problem. In the silence of my room, He whispered, "Celebrate!" After meditating on what this meant, I came to understand that every day, whether I am having a good day or not, I should celebrate the presence of God in my life. He has been with me since I was in the womb, and He has worked things out for me time after time. Because He promised to take care of me, worrying is not an option. In the midst of any struggle, celebrating His presence is the best option. One of my goals is to remain faithful and submitted to God so that Satan will not win in me, and I pray for my family that God will help them to have the same goal.

Those around us can benefit from our positive walk with God. We can choose to react to life in a way that leaves a heritage of love, faith, and hope.

Every saint has a past; every sinner, a future.
Oscar Wilde

The power of God is awesome! I'm not angry at anyone anymore. I am not holding unforgiveness against anyone. I am at peace with myself.

Meditate on how to love yourself with the same love God has for you. Then, and only then, can the command to love others as yourself bear lasting fruit.

*We are not who we **think** we are.*
*We are not who others **think** we are.*
*We really are who God **says** we are!*

PART 5

Strong Warnings

Stay alert! Watch out for your great enemy, the devil. He prowls around like a roaring lion, looking for someone to devour. Stand firm against him, and be strong in your faith. 1 Peter 5:8-9a

Chapter 20
Don't Lose Focus

Our spiritual enemy, Satan, works consistently to draw believers away from our godly calling by tempting our human nature to take precedence over God's spiritual leadership. If our reasoning takes over and produces a carnal response, we can move onto a path that will lead us away from what God desires. I call those human-reasoning paths "pitfalls." Following are some common pitfalls to avoid.

AVOID PARTICIPATING IN SELFISH MINISTRIES

There are no perfect people, so there are no perfect ministries. Therefore, areas of weakness can be found in any ministry. God has designed servant-leaders to oversee churches, so that ministries can be led by credible and godly men and women. If you are confident that the leaders of your church have a heart to serve God and people more than themselves, other small problems can be dealt with over time and not be a deterrent to the positive nature of the ministry. If you suspect the opposite, that your leaders are more concerned with their personal appeal in order to draw people and money, pray fervently to God for direction as to where to relocate. He would not have you waste precious time serving under selfish leaders. God desires to place each believer according to His will. If you are not sure that you are serving in the ministry of His choice, ask God for clarification.

AVOID THE MISUSE OF YOUR GIFTS

Everything belongs to God. Don't be foolish and use His gifts for selfish purposes. One way to avoid a misuse of God's gifts is to remain aware of your need to consistently be renewed in the spirit of your mind, according to what Ephesians 4:23 teaches. Otherwise you may hold on to the mindset you had before salvation.

Pride and arrogance are an assault against the sovereignty of God. Instead of building up the Body of Christ, pride and arrogance will work to tear it down and cause others to stumble. The evidence that you are submitted to God and on the right path is that His nature is growing in you. This process is spoken of as growing in the Fruit of the Spirit. According to Galatians 5:22-23a, maturing believers are growing in "love, joy, peace, patience, kindness, goodness, faithfulness, gentleness, and self-control." The proper use of gifts combined with the fruit of God's Spirit works to build up the Body of Christ and the world.

AVOID THE PITFALL OF BIGOTRY

Bigotry is defined as the "stubborn and complete intolerance of any creed, belief, or opinion that differs from one's own" (Dictionary.com). Bigotry is an ungodly behavior that is rooted in sin. Fortunately, believers have the power to overcome this selfish dictate of the flesh. Bigotry is grounded in hatred. A believer who is full of the love of God does not practice hatred against others, because His indwelling love cannot exist in the same space as hatred.

It is a travesty for bigotry to exist among church groups when their various doctrines collide. Wherever there is suspicion and distrust between Christian denominations, the love of God is not on display. It is implausible that those who claim to have the Spirit of God should have beliefs so vastly different that they cause division in the Body of Christ. There is only one Word of God. A proper understanding and application of Scripture brings unity among believers. God is love in action. Remember, it is a tactic of the devil to divide and conquer.

AVOID BEING POLARIZED BY POLITICAL AFFILIATIONS

In addition to groups being polarized along the lines of conflicting doctrinal beliefs, political polarity is also common and troublesome in many church groups. The Bible has this specific warning for believers:

> *Endure suffering along with me, as a good soldier of Christ Jesus. Soldiers don't get tied up in the affairs of civilian life, for then they cannot please the officer who enlisted them. 2 Timothy 2:3-4*

Politics is by nature a corrupt, dirty business. It is unwise for a believer to be so entangled with politics that he or she is drawn more to a political party than to the command of Scripture to not be entangled in worldly affairs. Politics should never negatively affect relationships among believers who may not share the same view about government issues.

Political affiliations should never be allowed to infiltrate church doctrine and plant a wedge between Christian brothers and sisters. Even though many politicians claim to be believers, the political realm in which they serve is worldly and manipulative. It is full of smoke and mirrors that are meant to deceive.

During His ministry on earth, Jesus didn't allow Himself to be drawn into Jewish or Roman politics. A believer's commitment should never be divided between the work of ministry and politics, no matter what secular cause is being touted. Any level of political polarization speaks of a problem with the level of commitment to Jesus. Those who allow themselves to be polarized by politics have most likely been divided out of the fear that God is not really in control. During an election, we don't know what is in the mind of God until He informs us. A believer should always pray to God for direction in all areas of life, even before casting a vote.

PART 6

The Marvelous Participation

Chapter 21
Summing It Up

So humble yourselves before God. James 4:7

The Apostle Paul passionately appeals to believers to walk closely with God in order to understand how to fit into the plan for which He designed us. Humility and trust put us in the position to answer and fulfill our calling. Submitting is not easy, especially when God calls us to rise above fear and focus on His power. Once we take courage and accept that there is a specific calling on our lives, God will awaken hunger in us to search for our place in His service. Finding it is an act of obedience. The satisfaction and joy that will come when you find your place of service cannot be measured. This is the best way to spend your precious time on earth. You will probably not know the depths of how you have blessed others until after you passed on into eternal life.

If you are not involved in the ministry for which God designed you, you are missing out on a marvelous experience. It is your free will that will drive this exploration, but the process will be assisted every step of the way by God because it is His desire for you.

Because many believers don't have a deep relationship with God they fail to understand how fearfully and wonderfully they are made. But if you accept this as truth and humbly submit, you will forge ahead and be amazed at how God will enable you to bless others. I implore you to let God have His way in you. Here is a wonderful paraphrase from the Apostle Paul's letter to the Ephesians:

> *Now God has us where he wants us, with all the time in this world and the next to shower grace and kindness upon us in Christ Jesus. Saving is all his idea, and all his work. All we do is trust him enough to let him do it. It's God's gift from start to finish! We don't play the major role. If we did, we'd probably go around bragging that we'd done the whole thing! No, we neither make nor save ourselves. God does both the making and saving. He creates each of us by Christ Jesus to join him in the work he does, the good work he has gotten ready for us to do, work we had better be doing. Ephesians 2:7-10 (The Message)*

You are God's masterpiece. You are what He has made. The "good work" in the previous Scripture refers to beneficial things planned specifically for you to do. "Planned for us long ago" means that even before you were born or saved, God had a plan for your life. The good works point both to living a righteous life and to fulfilling your place in the work of God.

He makes the whole body fit together perfectly. As each part does its own special work, it helps the other parts grow, so that the whole body is healthy and growing and full of love. Ephesians 4:16

Notice the phrase "as each part does its own special work." Paul is pointing to how our unique talents, skills, and abilities that the Holy Spirit anoints in each of us work for the good of the whole Body of Christ. Be encouraged that the Spirit of God will work supernaturally in you and enable you to work with Him. The spiritual gifts survey mentioned in Chapter 15 should help you see your top three gifts that God will fine-tune as you serve.

1 Corinthians gives us some vital information concerning spiritual gifts:

12:4 *There are different kinds of spiritual gifts* (not everybody has the same gift).

12:5 *There are different kinds of service* (various areas of ministry).

12:6 *God works in different ways* (He expresses His power and love in various ways).

12:7 *The anointed service we give are expressions of the Holy Spirit working among us for the common good.* (We help to meet the needs of one other)

12:8-10 (Various gifts are named.)

12:18 *God gifts each believer as it pleases Him, not as it pleases the person.*

I repeat, contrary to the belief of many church members, it is not the duty of pastors to carry the load of ministry. God planned that those with specific gifts should be used to train the members for ministry:

> *Now these are the gifts Christ gave to the church: the apostles, the prophets, the evangelists, and the pastors and teachers. Their responsibility is to equip God's people to do his work and build up the church, the body of Christ. This will continue until we all come to such unity in our faith and knowledge of God's Son that we will be mature in the Lord, measuring up to the full and complete standard of Christ. Ephesians 4:11-13*

YOU HAVE BEEN DESIGNED WITH A UNIQUE CALLING THAT ONLY YOU CAN FULFILL

Abbreviated List Of Gift Descriptions

From Mintools.com

APOSTLE: Eph. 4:11; 1 Cor. 12:28 - to be sent forth to new frontiers with the gospel, providing leadership over church bodies and maintaining authority over spiritual matters pertaining to the church (Greek Word: apostolos - 'apo'=from 'stello'=send; one sent forth)

CELIBACY: 1 Cor. 7:7,8 - to voluntarily remain single without regret and with the ability to maintain controlled sexual impulses so as to serve the Lord without distraction

DISCERNMENT: 1 Cor. 12:10 - to clearly distinguish truth from error by judging whether the behavior or teaching is from God, Satan, human error, or human power

EVANGELISM: Eph. 4:11 - to be a messenger of the good news of the Gospel (Greek Word: euaggelistes - preacher of *the* gospel; eu=well, angelos=message - messenger of good)

EXHORTATION: Rom. 12:8 - to come along side of someone with words of encouragement, comfort, consolation, and counsel to help them be all God wants them to be (Greek Word: paraklesis - calling to one's side)

FAITH: 1 Cor. 12:8-10 - to be firmly persuaded of God's power and promises to accomplish His will and purpose and to display such a confidence in Him and His Word that circumstances and obstacles do not shake that conviction

GIVING: Rom. 12:8 - to share what material resources you have with liberality and cheerfulness without thought of return

HEALINGS: 1 Cor. 12:9,28,30 - to be used as a means through which God makes people whole either physically, emotionally, mentally, or spiritually

HELPS: 1 Cor. 12:28 - to render support or assistance to others in the body so as to free them up for ministry

HOSPITALITY: 1 Pet. 4:9,10 - to warmly welcome people, even strangers, into one's home or church as a means of serving those in need of food or lodging (Greek Word: philoxenos - love of strangers; 'philos'=love; 'xenos'=stranger)

KNOWLEDGE: 1 Cor. 12:8 - to seek to learn as much about the Bible as possible through the gathering of much information and the analyzing of that data

LEADERSHIP: Rom. 12:8 - to stand before the people in such a way as to attend to the direction of the body with such care and diligence so as to motivate others to get involved in the accomplishment of these goals

MARTYRDOM: 1 Cor. 13:3 - to give over one's life to suffer or to be put to death for the cause of Christ

MERCY: Rom. 12:8 - to be sensitive toward those who are suffering, whether physically, mentally, or emotionally, so as to feel genuine sympathy with their misery, speaking words of compassion but more so caring for them with deeds of love to help alleviate their distress

MIRACLES: 1 Cor. 12:10,28 - to be enabled by God to perform mighty deeds which witnesses acknowledge to be of supernatural origin and means

MISSIONARY: Eph. 3:6-8 - to be able to minister in another culture

PASTOR: Eph. 4:11 - to be responsible for spiritually caring for, protecting, guiding, and feeding a group of believers entrusted to one's care

PROPHECY: Rom. 12:6; 1 Cor. 12:10; Eph. 4:11 - to speak forth the message of God to His people (Greek Word: prophetes - the forth-telling of the will of God; 'pro'=forth; 'phemi'=to speak)

SERVICE: Rom. 12:7 - to identify undone tasks in Gods work, however menial, and use available resources to get the job done (Greek Word: diakonia - deacon, attendant 'diako'=to run errands)

TEACHING: Rom. 12:7; 1 Cor. 12:28; Eph. 4:11 - to instruct others in the Bible in a logical, systematic way so as to communicate pertinent information for true understanding and growth

TONGUES: 1 Cor. 12:10; 14:27-28 - to speak in a language not previously learned so unbelievers can hear a message from God in their own language or the body be edified

THE INTERPRETATION OF TONGUES:
1 Cor. 12:10; 14:27, 28 - to translate the message of someone who has spoken in tongues

VOLUNTARY POVERTY: 1 Cor. 13:3 - to purposely live an impoverished lifestle to serve and aid others with your material resources

WISDOM: 1 Cor. 12:8 - to apply knowledge to life in such a way as to make spiritual truths quite relevant and practical in proper decision-making and daily life situations

Suggestions For Further Reading

The Holy Bible
(Some suggested versions are the New King James Version, the New International Version, the English Standard Version, and the New Living Translation)

Your Spiritual Gifts Can Help Your Church Grow
by C. Peter Wagner

Finding Your Spiritual Gifts Questionnaire: The Easy-to-Use, Self-Guided Questionnaire
by C. Peter Wagner

Discover Your Spiritual Gifts: The Easy-to-Use, Self-Guided Questionnaire That Helps You Identify and Understand Your Various God-Given Spiritual Gifts
by C. Peter Wagner

Personality Types: Using the Enneagram for Self-Discovery
by Don Richard Riso and Russ Hudson

The Wisdom of the Enneagram: The Complete Guide to Psychological and Spiritual Growth for the Nine Personality Types
by Don Richard Riso and Russ Hudson

Jesus Always
365 Devotionals by Sarah Young

www.ingramcontent.com/pod-product-compliance
Lightning Source LLC
Chambersburg PA
CBHW071703040426
42446CB00011B/1892